THE PEASANT WAR IN GERMANY

By
FREDERICK ENGELS

NEW YORK
INTERNATIONAL PUBLISHERS

With Introduction and Notes by D. Riazanov

Translated from the German by Moissaye J. Olgin

Copyright, 1926, by
INTERNATIONAL PUBLISHERS CO., Inc.
NEW EDITION, 1966

This Printing, 1976

ISBN 0-7178-0152-7

Library of Congress Catalog Card Number: 66-21949

Printed in the United States of America

CONTENTS

MARTIN LUTHER

Woodcut by
Lucas Cranach

THOMAS MUENZER

INTRODUCTION

Four hundred years have passed since the great Peasant War in Germany. It differs from similar peasant uprisings of the Fourteenth Century in Italy, France and England, in that these uprisings were of a more or less local character and were directed against the money economy then in the process of development, while the Peasant War, unfolding in the epoch of early capitalism which was creating a world market, was intimately related to the events of the Reformation. This more complex historic background, compared with the background of the Fourteenth Century, rendered more complex the class grouping whose struggle determined the whole course of the Peasant War. The rôle of proletarian elements also becomes more pronounced compared with earlier uprisings.

It was natural that, with the growth of a democratic movement in Germany, especially after the July Revolution in France, attention should be directed towards the study of the great Peasant War. A series of popular brochures and works examining individual phases of the movement made their appearance, and in 1841 there was published the monumental work of Zimmermann, which, to the present time, remains the most detailed narrative of the events of the Peasant War in Germany.[1]

It was also natural that the German communists, confronted with the necessity of determining how far the peasantry could be relied upon as a revolutionary factor, should have carefully studied the history of the Peasant War. Their attention was particularly drawn to the leaders of the Peasant War, one of whom was Thomas Muenzer. It is characteristic that as early as 1845, Engels, in one of his first articles for the Chartist "Northern Star," called the attention of the English workers to this "famous leader of the Peasant War of 1525," who, according to Engels, was a real democrat, and fought for real demands, not illusions.

Marx and Engels, who very soberly regarded the rôle of the peasantry in the realisation of a *social* revolution never underestimated its rôle as a revolutionary factor in the struggle against the large landowners and the feudal masters. They understood very well that the more the peasantry falls under the leadership of revolutionary classes which unite it, the more capable it is of general political actions. Led by the revolutionary proletariat, supporting its struggle against capitalism in the city and the village, the peasantry appeared to be a very important ally. This is why Marx and Engels, during the revolution of 1848-49, mercilessly exposed the cowardly conduct of the German bourgeoisie, which, currying favour with the Junkers and afraid of the proletariat, had refused to defend the interests of the peasantry.

It was with the aim of instructing the German bourgeois democracy that in 1850, Engels, supported by the factual material collected by the democrat, Zimmermann, wrote this splendid account of the German Peasant War. First, he gives a picture of the economic situation and of the class composition of Germany of that time. Then he shows how out of this soil sprang the various opposition groups with their programmes, and gives a colourful characterisation of Luther and Muenzer. The third chapter contains a brief history of the peasant uprisings in the German Empire from 1476 to 1517, that is, to the beginning of the Reformation. In the fourth chapter we have the history of the uprising of the nobility under the leadership of Franz von Sickingen and Ulrich von Hutten. The fifth and sixth chapters contain a narrative of the events of the Peasant War as such, with a detailed explanation of the main causes of the peasants' defeat. In the seventh and last chapters the significance of the Peasant War and its consequences in German history are explained.

Permeating the whole of Engels' work is the idea of the necessity of a merciless struggle against the feudal masters, the landlords. Only a radical abolition of all traces of feudal domination, he said, could create the most favourable conditions for the success of a proletarian revolution. In this respect Engels was in full harmony with Marx, who wrote to him later (August 16, 1856), "Everything in Germany will depend upon whether it will be possible to support the proletarian revolution by something like a second edition of the Peasant War. Only then will everything proceed well."

Quite different was the conception of Lassalle, who overestimated the significance of the uprising of the nobility, idealized Franz von Sickingen and Ulrich von Hutten, and treated the revolutionary movement of the lower plebeian strata too contemptuously. In his opinion, the Peasant War, notwithstanding its revolutionary appearance, was in reality a reactionary movement. "You all know," he said to the Berlin workers, "that the peasants killed the nobles and burned their castles, or, according to the prevailing habit, made them run the gauntlet. However, notwithstanding this revolutionary appearance, the movement was, in substance and principle, *reactionary*."

The Russian revolutionary populists, especially the adherents of Bakunin, often identified Lassalle's view of the peasants with the views of Marx and Engels. In this they followed Bakunin's lead, who wrote the following:

"Everybody knows that Lassalle repeatedly expressed the idea that the defeat of the peasant uprising in the Fourteenth Century and the strengthening and rapid growth of the bureaucratic state in Germany that followed it were a veritable triumph for the revolution." According to Bakunin, the German communists viewed all peasants as elements of reaction. "The fact is," he added, "that the Marxists cannot think otherwise; worshippers of state power at any price, they are bound to curse every people's revolution, especially a peasant revolution, which is anarchic by its very nature, and which proceeds directly to annihilate the state."

When Bakunin wrote these lines, there was already in existence the second edition of Engels' work on the Peasant War, with a new preface (1870), in which the inconsistency of Liebknecht and other contemporary German social-democrats on the agrarian question was criticised. In 1875, the third edition appeared, with an addendum which emphasised still more the sharp difference between the views of Marx and Engels on the one hand, and Lassalle on the other.

It must be noted that in the last years of his life, Engels devoted much labour to the study of the Peasant War, and was about to recast his old work.

In 1882 he wrote a special addition to his *Socialism, Utopian and Scientific,* devoted to the history of the German peasantry. On December 31, 1884, he wrote to Sorge: "I am subjecting my *Peasant War* to radical reconstruction. It is going to become a cornerstone of German history. It is a great piece of work. All the preliminary work is almost ready."

The work of preparing the second and third volumes of *Capital* for publication, prevented him from carrying out his plan. In July, 1893, he wrote to Mehring, "If I succeed in reconstructing anew the historic introduction to my *Peasant War,* which I hope will be possible during this winter, I will give there an exposition of my views" [concerning the conditions of the breaking up of Germany and the causes of the defeat of the German bourgeois revolution of the Sixteenth Century].

When Kautsky was writing his book on the forerunners of modern socialism—it appeared in parts—Engels wrote to him on May 21, 1895: "Of your book, I can tell you that the further it proceeds, the better it becomes. Compared with the original plan, Plato and early Christianity are not sufficiently worked out. The mediæval sects are much better, and the later ones, more so. Best of all are the Taborites, Muenzer, and the Anabaptists. I have learned much from your book. For my recasting of the *Peasant War,* it is an indispensable preliminary work.

"In my judgment, there are only two considerable faults:

"(1) A very insufficient insight into the development and the rôle of those elements entirely outside of the feudal hierarchy, which are déclassé, occupying almost the place of pariahs; elements that form the lowest stratum of the population of every mediæval city, without rights and outside the rural community, the feudal dependence, the guild bonds. This is difficult, but it is the *chief foundation,* since gradually, with the decomposition of feudal relations, out of this stratum develops the predecessor of the proletariat which, in 1789, in the faubourgs of Paris, made the revolution. You speak of the proletarians, but this expression is not entirely exact; when you count among your 'proletarians' the weavers, whose significance you picture very correctly, you may rightly do so, only beginning from that epoch when the déclassé non-guild journeyman weavers made their appearance and only in so far as the latter were in existence. Much work is still required in this connection.

"(2) You have not sufficiently taken into account the situation of the world market, in so far as one could speak of such a market at that time, and the international economic situation of Germany at the end of the Fifteenth Century. However, only this situation explains why the bourgeois-plebeian movement under a religious cloak, having suffered defeat in England, the Netherlands and Bohemia, could achieve a measure of success in Germany in the Sixteenth Century. This was due to its religious cloak, whereas the success of its bourgeois *contents* was reserved for the following century and for the countries which had utilized the development of the world market that had in the meantime taken another direction, namely, Holland and England. It is a great subject, which I hope to be able to treat briefly in the *Peasant War*, if I only succeed in taking it up!"

Death—Engels died several days after the writing of this letter (August 5, 1895)—prevented him from completing this work.   D. RIAZANOV.

Moscow, July, 1925.

AUTHOR'S PREFACE TO THE SECOND EDITION

THIS work was written in London in the summer of 1850, under the vivid impression of the counter-revolution that had just been completed. It appeared in 1850 in the fifth and sixth issues of the *Neue Rheinische Zeitung*, a political economic review edited by Karl Marx in Hamburg. My political friends in Germany desire to see it in book form, and I hereby fulfil that desire, since, unfortunately, it still has the interest of timeliness.

The work does not pretend to present independently collected material. Quite the contrary, all the material relating to the peasant revolts and to Thomas Muenzer has been taken from Zimmermann whose book, although showing gaps here and there, is still the best presentation of the facts. Moreover, old Zimmermann enjoyed his subject. The same revolutionary instinct which makes him here the advocate of the oppressed classes, made him later one of the best in the extreme left wing of Frankfurt.

If, nevertheless, the Zimmermann representation lacks internal coherence; if it does not succeed in showing the religious and political controversies of that epoch as a reflection of the class struggles that were taking place simultaneously; if it sees in the class struggles only oppressors and oppressed, good and evil, and the final victory of evil; if its insight into social conditions which determined both the outbreak and the outcome of the struggle is extremely poor, it was the fault of the time in which that book came into existence. Nevertheless, for its time, and among the German idealistic works on history, it stands out as written in a very realistic vein.

This book, while giving the historic course of the struggle only in its outlines, undertakes to explain the origin of the peasant wars, the attitude of the various parties which appear in the war, the political and religious theories through which those parties strove to make clear to themselves their position; and finally, the result of the struggle as determined by the historical-social conditions of life, to show the political constitution of Germany of that time, the revolt against it; and to prove that the political and religious theories were not the causes, but the result of that stage in the development of agriculture, industry, land and waterways, commerce and finance, which then existed in Germany. This, the only materialistic conception of history, originates, not from myself but from Marx, and can be found in his works on the French Revolution of 1848-9, published in the same review, and in his *Eighteenth Brumaire of Louis Bonaparte.*

The parallel between the German Revolutions of 1525 and of 1848-9 was too obvious to be left entirely without attention. However, together with an identity of events in both cases, as for instance, the suppression of one local revolt after the other by the army of the princes, together with a sometimes comic similitude in the behaviour of the city middle-class, the difference is quite clear.

"Who profited by the Revolution of 1525? The princes. Who profited by the Revolution of 1848? The big princes, Austria and Prussia. Behind the princes of 1525 there stood the lower middle-class of the cities, held chained by means of taxation. Behind the big princes of 1850, there stood the modern big bourgeoisie, quickly subjugating them by means of the State debt. Behind the big bourgeoisie stand the proletarians."

I am sorry to state that in this paragraph too much honour was given to the German bourgeoisie. True, it had the opportunity of "quickly subjugating" the monarchy by means of the State debt. Never did it avail itself of this opportunity.

Austria fell as a boon into the lap of the bourgeoisie after the war of 1866, but the bourgeoisie does not understand how to govern. It is powerless and inefficient in everything. Only one thing is it capable of doing: to storm against the workers as soon as they begin to stir. It remains at the helm only because the Hungarians need it.

And in Prussia? True, the State debt has increased by leaps and bounds. The deficit has become a permanent feature. The State expenditures keep growing, year in and year out. The bourgeoisie have a majority in the Chamber. No taxes can be increased and no debts incurred without their consent. But where is their power in the State? It was only a couple of months ago, when a deficit was looming, that again they found themselves in the most favourable position. They could have gained considerable concessions by persevering. What was their reaction? They considered it a sufficient concession when the Government *allowed* them to lay at its feet nine millions, not for one year alone, but to be collected indefinitely every year.

I do not want to blame the "national liberals" of the Chamber more than is their due. I know they have been forsaken by those who stand behind them, by the mass of the bourgeoisie. This mass does not wish to govern. 1848 is still in its bones.

Why the German bourgeoisie has developed this remarkable trait, will be discussed later.

In general, however, the above quotation has proved perfectly true. Beginning from 1850, the small States were in constant retreat, serving only as levers for Prussian and Austrian intrigues. Austria and Prussia were engaged in ever-stronger struggles for supremacy. Finally, the fearful clash of 1866 took place. Austria, retaining all its provinces, subjugated, directly and indirectly, the entire north of Prussia, while leaving the fate of the three southern States in the air.

In all these grand activities of the States, only the following are of particular importance for the German working class:

First, that universal suffrage has given the workers the power to be directly represented in the legislative assemblies.

Second, that Prussia has set a good example by swallowing three crowns by the grace of God. That after this operation her own crown is maintained by the grace of God as pure as she claims it to be, not even the national liberals believe any more.

Third, that there is only one serious enemy of the Revolution in Germany at the present time—the Prussian government.

Fourth, that the Austro-Germans will now be compelled to ask themselves what they wish to be, Germans or Austrians; whom they wish to adhere to, to Germany or her extraordinary transleithanian appendages. It has been obvious for a long time that they will have to give up one or the other. Still, this has been continually glossed over by the petty-bourgeois democracy.

As to other important controversies concerning 1866 which were threshed out between the "national-liberals" and the people's party *ad nauseam,* coming years will show that the two standpoints fought so bitterly simply because they were the opposite poles of the same stupidity.

In the social conditions of Germany, the year 1866 has changed almost nothing. A few bourgeois reforms: uniform measures and weights, freedom of movement, freedom of trade, etc.,—all within limits befitting bureaucracy, do not even come up to that of which other western European countries have been in possession for a long while, and leaves the main evil, the system of bureaucratic concessions, unshaken. As to the proletariat, the freedom of movement, and of citizenship, the abolition of passports and other such legislation is made illusory by the current police practice.

What is much more important than the grand manœuvres of the State in 1866 is the growth of German industry and commerce, of the railways, the telegraph, and ocean steamship navigation since 1848. This progress may be lagging behind that of England or even France, but it is unheard of for Germany, and has done more in twenty years than would have been previously possible in a century. Germany has been drawn, earnestly and irrevocably, into world commerce. Capital invested in industry has multiplied rapidly. The position of the bourgeoisie has improved accordingly. The surest sign of industrial prosperity—speculation—has blossomed richly, princes and dukes being chained to its triumphal chariot. German capital is now constructing Russian and Rumanian railways, whereas, only fifteen years ago, the German railways went a-begging to English entrepreneurs. How, then, is it possible that the bourgeoisie has not conquered political power, that it behaves in so cowardly a manner toward the government?

It is the misfortune of the German bourgeoisie to have come too late,—quite in accordance with the beloved German tradition. The period of its ascendancy coincides with the time when the bourgeoisie of the other western European countries is politically on the downward path. In England, the bourgeoisie could place its real representative, Bright, into the government only by extending the franchise which in the long run is bound to put an end to its very domination. In France, the bourgeoisie, which for two years only, 1849-50, had held power as a class under the republican régime, was able to continue its social existence only by transferring its power to Louis Bonaparte and the army. Under present conditions of enormously increased interdependence of the three most progressive European countries, it is no more possible for the German bourgeoisie extensively to utilize its political power while the same class has outlived itself in England and France. It is a peculiarity of the bourgeoisie, distinguishing it from all other classes, that a point is being reached in its development after which every increase in its power, that is, every enlargement of its capital, only tends to make it more and more incapable of retaining political dominance. *"Behind the big bourgeoisie stand the proletarians."* In the degree as the bourgeoisie develops its industry, its commerce, and its means of communication, it also produces the proletariat. At a certain point, which must not necessarily appear simultaneously and on the same stage of development everywhere, it begins to note that this, its second self, has outgrown it. From then on, it loses the power for exclusive political dominance. It looks for allies with whom to share its authority, or to whom to cede all power, as circumstances may demand.

In Germany, this turning point came for the bourgeoisie as early as 1848. The bourgeoisie became frightened, not so much by the German, as by the French proletariat. The battle of June, 1848, in Paris, showed the bourgeoisie what could be expected. The German proletariat was restless enough to prove to the bourgeoisie that the seed of revolution had been sown also in German soil. From that day, the edge of bourgeois political action was broken. The bourgeoisie looked around for allies. It sold itself to them regardless of price, and there it remains.

These allies are all of a reactionary turn. It is the king's power, with his army and his bureaucracy; it is the big feudal nobility; it is the smaller Junker; it is even the clergy. The bourgeoisie has made so many compacts and unions with all of them to save its dear skin, that now it has nothing more to barter. And the more the proletariat developed, the more it began to feel as a class and to act as one, the feebler became the bourgeoisie. When the astonishingly bad strategy of the Prussians triumphed over the astonishingly worse strategy of the Austrians at Sadowa, it was difficult to say who gave a deeper sigh of relief, the Prussian bourgeois, who was a partner to the defeat at Sadowa, or his Austrian colleague.

Our upper middle-class of 1870 acted in the same fashion as did the moderate middle-class of 1525. As to the small bourgeoisie, the master artisans and merchants, they remain unchanged. They hope to climb up to the big bourgeoisie, and they are fearful lest they be pushed down into the ranks of the proletariat. Between fear and hope, they will in times of struggle seek to save their precious skin and to join the victors when the struggle is over. Such is their nature.

The social and political activities of the proletariat have kept pace with the rapid growth of industry since 1848. The rôle of the German workers, as expressed in their trade unions, their associations, political organisations and public meetings, at elections, and in the so-called Reichstag, is alone a sufficient indication of the transformation which came over Germany in the last twenty years. It is to the credit of the German workers that *they alone* have managed to send workers and workers' representatives into the Parliament—a feat which neither the French nor the English had hitherto accomplished.

Still, even the proletariat shows some resemblance to 1525. The class of the population which entirely and permanently depends on wages is now, as then, a minority of the German people. This class is also compelled to seek allies. The latter can be found only among the petty bourgeoisie, the low grade proletariat of the cities, the small peasants, and the wage-workers of the land.

The petty bourgeoisie has been mentioned above. This class is entirely unreliable except when a victory has been won. Then its noise in the beer saloons is without limit. Nevertheless, there are good elements among it, who, of their own accord, follow the workers.

The *lumpenproletariat*, this scum of the decaying elements of all classes, which establishes headquarters in all the big cities, is the worst of all possible allies. It is an absolutely venal, an absolutely brazen crew. If the French workers, in the course of the Revolution, inscribed on the houses: *Mort aux voleurs!* (Death to the thieves!) and even shot down many, they did it, not out of enthusiasm for property, but because they rightly considered it necessary to hold that band at arm's length. Every leader of the workers who utilises these gutter-proletarians as guards or supports, proves himself by this action alone a traitor to the movement.

The small peasants (bigger peasants belong to the bourgeoisie) are not homogeneous. They are either in serfdom bound to their lords and masters, and inasmuch as the bourgeoisie has failed to do its duty in freeing those people from serfdom, it will not be difficult to convince them that salvation, for them, can be expected only from the working class; or they are tenants, whose situation is almost equal to that of the Irish. Rents are so high that even in times of normal crops the peasant and his family can hardly eke out a bare existence; when the crops are bad, he virtually starves. When he is unable to pay his rent, he is entirely at the mercy of the landlord. The bourgeoisie thinks of relief only under compulsion. Where, then, should the tenants look for relief outside of the workers?

There is another group of peasants, those who own a small piece of land. In most cases they are so burdened with mortgages that their dependence upon the usurer is equal to the dependence of the tenant upon the landlord. What they earn is practically a meagre wage, which, since good and bad crops alternate, is highly uncertain. These people cannot have the least hope of getting anything out of the bourgeoisie, because it is the bourgeoisie, the capitalist usurers, that squeeze the life-blood out of them. Still, the peasants cling to their property, though in reality it does not belong to them, but to the usurers. It will be necessary to make it clear to these people that only when a government of the people will have transformed all mortgages into a debt to the State, and thereby lowered the rent, will they be able to free themselves from the usurer. This, however, can be accomplished only by the working class.

Wherever middle and large land ownership prevails, the wage-workers of the land form the most numerous class. This is the case throughout the entire north and east of Germany, and it is here that the industrial workers of the city find their most numerous and natural allies. In the same way as the capitalist is opposed to the industrial worker, the large landowner or large tenant is opposed to the wage-workers of the land. The measures that help the one must also help the other. The industrial workers can free themselves only by turning the capital of the bourgeoisie, that is, the raw materials, machines and tools, the foodstuffs necessary for production, into social property, their own property, to be used by them in common. Similarly, the wage-workers of the land can be freed from their hideous misery only when the main object of their work, the land itself, will be withdrawn from the private property of the large peasants and still larger feudal masters, and transformed into social property to be cultivated by an association of land workers on a common basis. And here we come to the famous decision of the International Socialist Congress in Basle: That it is in the interest of society to transform property on land into common national property. This decision was made primarily for those countries where there is large land ownership, with large agricultural enterprises, with one master and many wage-workers in every estate. It is these conditions that still prevail in Germany, and next to England, the decision was *most timely* for Germany. The agricultural proletariat, the wage-workers of the land, is the class from which the bulk of the armies of the princes is being recruited. It is the class which, thanks to universal suffrage, sends into Parliament the great mass of feudal masters and Junkers. However, it is also the class nearest to the industrial workers of the city. It shares their conditions of living, and it is still deeper steeped in misery than the city workers. This class, powerless because split and scattered, but possessing a hidden power which is so well known to the government and nobility that they purposely allow the schools to deteriorate in order that the rural population should remain unenlightened, must be called to life and drawn into the movement. This is the most urgent task of the German labour movement. From the day when the mass of the workers of the land have learned to understand their own interests, a reactionary, feudal, bureaucratic or bourgeois government in Germany becomes an impossibility.

ADDENDUM TO PREFACE TO THE SECOND EDITION

THE preceding lines were written over four years ago, but they are valid also at present. What was true after Sadowa and the partition of Germany, is being confirmed also after Sedan and the erection of the Holy German Empire of Prussian nationality. Little indeed are the "world shaking" activities of the States in the realm of so-called big politics in a position to change the trend of historic development.

What these grand activities of the States *are* in a position to accomplish is to hasten the tempo of historic movement. In this respect, the originators of the above-mentioned "world-shaking" events have made involuntary successes which to themselves appear highly undesirable, but which, however, they must take into the bargain, for better or worse.

Already the war of 1866 had shaken the old Prussia to its foundations. After 1848 it was difficult to bring the rebellious industrial element of the western provinces, bourgeois as well as proletarian, under the old discipline. Still, somehow, this was accomplished, and the interests of the Junkers of the eastern provinces, together with those of the army, again became dominant in the State. In 1866 almost all the northwest of Germany became Prussian. Besides the incurable moral injury to the Prussian crown, by the fact that it had swallowed up three other crowns by the grace of God, the centre of gravity of the monarchy had moved considerably westward. The four million Rhine-landers and Westphalians were reinforced, first, by four million Germans annexed through the North German Alliance directly, and then by six million annexed indirectly. In 1870, however, eight million southwest Germans were added, so that, in the "new monarchy," the fourteen and a half million old Prussians (all the six East Elbian provinces, among them, two million Poles) were opposed by twenty-five million who had long outgrown the old Prussian junker feudalism. So it happened that the very victories of the Prussian army displaced the entire foundation of the Prussian State edifice; the junker dominance became ever more intolerable, even for the government itself. At the same time, however, the struggle between the bourgeoisie and the workers made inevitable by the impetuous growth of industry, relegated to the background the struggle between junkers and bourgeoisie, so that the inner social foundations of the old State suffered a complete transformation. Ever since 1840, the condition making possible the existence of the slowly rotting monarchy was the struggle between nobility and bourgeoisie, wherein the monarchy retained equilibrium. From the moment, however, when it was no more a question of protecting the nobility against the onslaught of the bourgeoisie, but of protecting all propertied classes against the onslaught of the working-class, the absolute monarchy had to turn to that form of state which was expressly devised for this specific purpose,—the Bonapartist monarchy. This change of Prussia towards Bonapartism I have discussed in another place (*Wohnungsfrage*). What I did not stress there, and what is very important in this connection, is that this change was the greatest progress made by Prussia after 1848, which only shows how backward Prussia was in point of modern development. It is a fact that the Prussian State still was a semi-feudal State, whereas Bonapartism is, at all events, a modern form of state which presupposes the abolition of feudalism. Thus Prussia must decide to do away with its numerous remnants of feudalism, to sacrifice its junkerdom as such. This, naturally, is being done in the mildest possible form, and under the tune of the favourite melody, "Always slowly forward." An example of such "reform" work is the notorious organisation of districts, which, removing the feudal privileges of the individual Junker in relation to his estate, restores them as special privileges of the big landowners in relation to the entire district. The substance remains, it being only translated from the feudal into the bourgeois dialect. The old Prussian Junker is forcibly being transformed into something akin to the English squire. He need not have offered so much resistance, because the one is just as foolish as the other.

Thus it was the peculiar feat of Prussia not only to culminate, by the end of this century, her bourgeois revolution begun in 1808-13 and continued in 1848, but to culminate it in the present form of Bonapartism. If everything goes well, and the world remains nice and quiet, and we all become old enough, we can still perhaps live to see—about 1900—the government of Prussia actually relinquishing all feudal institutions, and Prussia finally reaching a point where France stood in 1792.

Speaking positively, the abolition of feudalism means the introduction of bourgeois conditions. In the measure as the privileges of the nobility fall, legislation becomes more and more bourgeois. Here, again, we meet with the chief point at issue, the attitude of the German bourgeoisie towards the government. We have seen that the government is compelled to introduce these slow and petty reforms, but in its relation to the bourgeoisie, the government portrays these small concessions as sacrifices in favour of the bourgeoisie, as concessions yielded by the crown with difficulty and pain, and for which the bourgeoisie must, in return, yield something to :he government. The bourgeoisie, on the other hand, though quite aware of this state of affairs, allows itself to be fooled. This is the source of the tacit agreement which is the basis of all Reichstag and Chamber debates. On the one hand, the government reforms the laws at a snail pace tempo in the interests of the bourgeoisie; it removes the impediments to industry emanating from the multiplicity of small states; it creates unity of coinage, of measures and weights; it gives freedom of trade, etc.; it grants the freedom of movement; it puts the working power of Germany at the unlimited disposal of capital; it creates favourable conditions for trade and speculation. On the other hand, the bourgeoisie leaves in the hands of the government all actual political power; it votes taxes, loans and recruits; it helps to frame all new reform laws in a way that the old police power over undesirable individuals shall remain in full force. The bourgeoisie buys its gradual social emancipation for the price of immediate renunciation of its own political power. Naturally, the motive which makes such agreement acceptable to the bourgeoisie is not the fear of the government but the fear of the proletariat.

Miserable as the bourgeoisie appears in the political realm, it cannot be denied that as far as industry and commerce are concerned, the bourgeoisie fulfils its historic duty. The growth of industry and commerce mentioned already in the introduction to the second edition has been going on with even greater vigour. What has taken place in the Rhenish-Westphalian industrial region since 1869, is unprecedented for Germany, and it reminds one of the rapid growth in the English manufacturing districts at the beginning of this century. The same thing will happen in Saxony and Upper Silesia, in Berlin, Hanover, and the southern States. At last we have world trade, a really big industry, and a really modern bourgeoisie. But we have also had a real crisis, and we have a truly mighty proletariat. For the future historian of Germany, the battle roar of 1859-64 on the field of Spicheren, Mars la Tour, Sedan, and the rest, will be of much less importance than the unpretentious, quiet, and constantly forward-moving development of the German proletariat. Immediately after 1870, the German workers stood before a grave trial— the Bonapartist war provocation and its natural sequence, the general national enthusiasm in Germany. The German workers did not allow themselves to be illusioned for a moment. Not a trace of national chauvinism made itself manifest among them. In the midst of a mania for victory, they remained cool, demanding "equitable peace with the French Republic and no annexations," and not even the state of siege was in a position to silence them. No glory of battle, no phraseology of German "imperial magnificence" attracted them. Their sole aim remained the liberation of the entire European proletariat. We may say with full assurance that in no country have the workers stood such a difficult test with such splendid results.

The state of siege of wartime was followed by trials for treason, *lèse majesté,* and contempt of officers and by ever increasing police atrocities practised in peace time. The *Volksstaat* had three or four editors in prison simultaneously; the other papers, in the same ratio. Every known party speaker had to face court at least once a year, and was usually convicted. Deportations, confiscations, suppressions of meetings rapidly followed one another, but all to no avail. The place of every prisoner or deportee was immediately filled by another. For one suppressed gathering, two others were substituted, wearing out arbitrary police power in one locality after the other by endurance and strict conformity to the law. Persecution defeated its own purpose. Far from breaking the workers' party or even bending it, it attracted ever new recruits, and strengthened the organisation. In their struggle against the authorities and the individual bourgeois, the workers manifested an intellectual and moral superiority. Particularly in their conflicts with the employers of labour did they show that they, the workers, were now the educated class, while the capitalists were dupes. In their fights, a sense of humour prevailed, showing how sure they were of their cause, and how superior they felt. A struggle thus conducted on historically prepared soil must yield great results. The success of the January (1874) elections stood out, unique in the history of the modern labour movement, and the astonishment aroused by them throughout Europe was perfectly deserved.

The German workers have two important advantages compared with the rest of Europe. First, they belong to the most theoretical people of Europe; second, they have retained that sense of theory which the so-called "educated" people of Germany have totally lost. Without German philosophy, particularly that of Hegel, German scientific Socialism (the only scientific Socialism extant) would never have come into existence. Without a sense for theory, scientific Socialism would have never become blood and tissue of the workers. What an enormous advantage this is, may be seen on the one hand from the indifference of the English labour movement towards all theory, which is one of the reasons why it moves so slowly in spite of the splendid organisation of the individual unions; on the other hand, from the mischief and confusion created by Proudhonism in its original form among the Frenchmen and Belgians, and in its caricature form, as presented by Bakunin, among the Spaniards and Italians.

The second advantage is that, chronologically speaking, the Germans were the last to appear in the labour movement. In the same manner as German theoretical Socialism will never forget that it rests on the shoulders of Saint Simon, Fourier and Owen, the three who, in spite of their fantastic notions and Utopianism, belonged to the most significant heads of all time and whose genius anticipated numerous things the correctness of which can now be proved in a scientific way, so the practical German labour movement must never forget that it has developed on the shoulders of the English and French movements, that it had utilised their experience, acquired at a heavy price, and that for this reason it was in a position to avoid their mistakes which in their time were unavoidable. Without the English trade unions and the French political workers' struggles preceding the German labour movement, without the mighty impulse given by the Paris Commune, where would we now be?

It must be said to the credit of the German workers that they have utilised the advantages of their situation with rare understanding. For the first time in the history of the labour movement the struggle is being so conducted that its three sides, the theoretical, the political and the practical economical (opposition to the capitalists), form one harmonious and well-planned entity. In this concentric attack, as it were, lies the strength and invincibility of the German movement.

It is due to this advantageous situation on the one hand, to the insular peculiarities of the British, and to the cruel suppression of the French movements on the other, that for the present moment the German workers form the vanguard of the proletarian struggle. How long events will allow them to occupy this post of honour cannot be foreseen. But as long as they are placed in it, let us hope that they will discharge their duties in the proper manner. It is the specific duty of the leaders to gain an ever clearer understanding of the theoretical problems, to free themselves more and more from the influence of traditional phrases inherited from the old conception of the world, and constantly to keep in mind that Socialism, having become a science, demands the same treatment as every other science—it must be studied. The task of the leaders will be to bring understanding, thus acquired and clarified, to the working masses, to spread it with increased enthusiasm, to close the ranks of the party organisations and of the labour unions with ever greater energy. The votes cast in favour of the Socialists last January may represent considerable strength, but they still are far from being the majority of the German working class; and encouraging as may be the successes of the propaganda among the rural population, more remains to be done in this field. The slogan is not to flinch in the struggle. The task is to wrest from the enemy's hands one seat after the other, one electoral district after the other. In the first place, however, it is necessary to retain a real international spirit which permits of no chauvinism, which joyfully greets each new step of the proletarian movement, no matter in which nation it is made. If the German workers proceed in this way, they may not march exactly at the head of the movement—it is not in the interest of the movement that the workers of one country should march at the head of all—but they will occupy an honourable place on the battle line, and they will stand armed for battle when other unexpected grave trials or momentous events will demand heightened courage, heightened determination, and the will to act.

FRIEDRICH ENGELS.

London, July 1, 1874.

THE PEASANT WAR
IN GERMANY

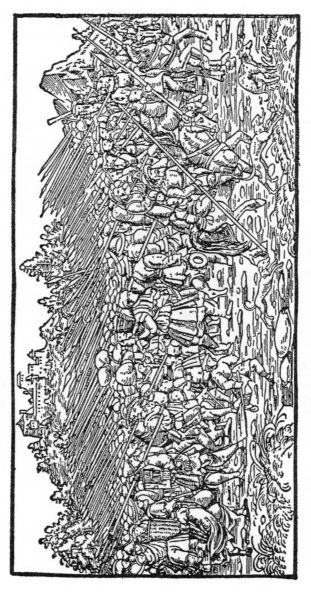

PEASANT TROOPS ON THE MARCH

THE PEASANT WAR
IN GERMANY

CHAPTER I

THE German people are by no means lacking in revolutionary tradition. There were times when Germany produced characters that could match the best men in the revolutions of other countries; when the German people manifested an endurance and energy which, in a centralised nation, would have brought the most magnificent results; when the German peasants and plebeians were pregnant with ideas and plans which often made their descendants shudder.

In contrast to present-day enfeeblement which appears everywhere after two years of struggle (since 1848) it is timely to present once more to the German people those awkward but powerful and tenacious figures of the great peasant war. Three centuries have flown by since then, and many a thing has changed; still the peasant war is not as far removed from our present-day struggles as it would seem, and the opponents we have to encounter remain essentially the same. Those classes and fractions of classes which everywhere betrayed 1848 and 1849, can be found in the rôle of traitors as early as 1525, though on a lower level of development. And if the robust vandalism of the peasant wars appeared in the movement of the last years only sporadically, in the Odenwald, in the Black Forest, in Silesia, it by no means shows a superiority of the modern insurrection.

Let us first review briefly the situation in Germany at the beginning of the Sixteenth Century.

German industry had gone through a considerable process of growth in the Fourteenth and Fifteenth Centuries. The local industry of the feudal countryside was superseded by the guild organisation of production in the cities, which produced for wider circles and even for remote markets. Weaving of crude woollen stuffs and linens had become a well-established, ramified branch of industry, and even finer woollen and linen fabrics, as well as silks, were already being produced in Augsburg. Outside of the art of weaving, there had arisen those branches of industry, which, approaching the finer arts, were nurtured by the demands for luxuries on the part of the ecclesiastic and lay lords of the late mediæval epoch: gold- and silver-smithing, sculpture and wood-carving, etching and wood-engraving, armour-making, medal-engraving, wood-turning, etc., etc. A series of more or less important discoveries culminating in the invention of gunpowder and printing had considerably aided the development of the crafts. Commerce kept pace with industry. The Hanseatic League, through its century-long monopoly of sea navigation, had brought about the emergence of the entire north of Germany out of mediæval barbarism; and even when, after the end of the Sixteenth Century, the Hanseatic League had begun to succumb to the competition of the English and the Dutch, the great highway of commerce from India to the north still lay through Germany, Vasco da Gama's discoveries notwithstanding. Augsburg still remained the great point of concentration for Italian silks, Indian spices, and all Levantine products. The cities of upper Germany, namely, Augsburg and Nuernberg, were the centres of opulence and luxury remarkable for that time. The production of raw materials had equally progressed. The German miners of the Fifteenth Century had been the most skilful in the world, and agriculture was also shaken out of its mediæval crudity through the blossoming forth of the cities. Not only had large stretches of land been put under cultivation, but dye plants and other imported cultures had been introduced, which in turn had a favourable influence on agriculture as a whole.

Still, the progress of national production in Germany had not kept pace with the progress of other countries. Agriculture lagged far behind that of England and Holland. Industry lagged far behind the Italian, Flemish and English, and as to sea navigation, the English, and especially the Dutch, were already driving the Germans out of the field. The population was still very sparse. Civilisation in Germany existed only in spots, around the centres of industry and commerce; but even the interests of these individual centres diverged widely, with hardly any point of contact. The trade relations and markets of the South differed from those of the North; the East and the West had almost no intercourse. No city had grown to become the industrial and commercial point of gravity for the whole country, such as London was for England. Internal communication was almost exclusively confined to coastwise and river navigation and to a few large commercial highways, like those from Augsburg and Nuernberg through Cologne to the Netherlands, and through Erfurt to the North. Away from the rivers and highways of commerce there was a number of smaller cities which, excluded from the great trade centres, continued a sluggish existence under conditions of late mediæval times, consuming few non-local articles, and yielding few products for export. Of the rural population, only the nobility came into contact with wide circles and new wants; the mass of the peasants never overstepped the boundaries of local relations and local outlook.

While in England, as well as in France, the rise of commerce and industry had brought about a linking of interests over the entire country, the political centralisation of Germany had succeeded only in the grouping of interests according to provinces and around purely local centres. This meant political decentralisation which later gained momentum through the exclusion of Germany from world commerce. In the degree as the purely feudal empire was falling apart, bonds of unity were becoming weakened, great feudal vassals were turning into almost independent princes, and cities of the empire on the one hand, the knights of the empire on the other, were forming alliances either against each other, or against the princes or the emperor. The imperial power, now uncertain as to its own position, vacillated between the various elements opposing the empire, and was constantly losing authority; the attempt at centralisation, in the manner of Louis XI,[2] brought about nothing but the holding together of the Austrian hereditary lands, this in spite of all intrigues and violent actions. The final winners, who could not help winning in this confusion, in this helter-skelter of numerous conflicts, were the representatives of centralisation amidst disunion, the representatives of local and provincial centralisation, the princes, beside whom the emperor gradually became no more than a prince among princes.

Under these conditions the situation of the classes emerging from mediæval times had considerably changed. New classes had been formed besides the old ones.

Out of the old nobility came the princes. Already they were almost independent of the emperor, and possessed the major part of sovereign rights. They declared war and made peace of their own accord, they maintained standing armies, called local councils, and levied taxes. They had already drawn a large part of the lower nobility and cities under their lordly power; they did everything in their power to incorporate in their lands all the rest of the cities and baronies which still remained under the empire. Towards such cities and baronies they appeared in the rôle of centralisers, while as far as the imperial power was concerned, they were the decentralising factor. Internally, their reign was already autocratic, they called the estates only when they could not do without them. They imposed taxes, and collected money whenever they saw fit. The right of the estates to ratify taxes was seldom recognised, and still more seldom practised. And even when they were called, the princes ordinarily had a majority, thanks to the knights and the prelates which were the two estates freed from taxes, participating, nevertheless, in their consumption. The need of the princes for money grew with the taste for luxuries, with the increase of the courts and the standing armies, with the mounting costs of administration. The taxes were becoming more and more oppressive. The cities being in most cases protected against them by privileges, the entire weight of the tax burden fell upon the peasants, those under the princes themselves, as well as the serfs and bondsmen of the knights bound by vassalage to the princes; wherever direct taxation was insufficient, indirect taxes were introduced; the most skilful machinations of the art of finance were utilised to fill the gaping holes of the fiscal system. When nothing else availed, when there was nothing to pawn and no free imperial city was willing to grant credit any longer, one resorted to coin manipulations of the basest kind, one coined depreciated money, one set a higher or lower rate of legal tender most convenient for the prince. Trading in city and other privileges, subsequently to be taken away by force, in order that they might again be sold, seizing every attempt at opposition as an excuse for incendiarism and robbery of every kind, etc., etc., were lucrative and quite ordinary sources of income for the princes of those times. The administration of justice was also a constant and not unimportant article of trade for the princes. In brief, the subjects who, besides the princes, had to satisfy the private appetites of their magistrates and bailiffs as well, were enjoying the full taste of the "fatherly" system. Of the mediæval feudal hierarchy, the knighthood of moderate possessions had almost entirely disappeared; it had either climbed up to the position of independence of small princes, or it had sunk into the ranks of the lower nobility. The lower nobility, the knighthood, was fast moving towards extinction. A large portion of it had already become pauperised, and lived on its services to the princes, either in military or in civil capacity; another portion was bound by vassalage to the sovereignty of the prince; a very small portion was directly under the empire. The development of military science, the rising importance of infantry, the spread of firearms, had dwarfed their military importance as heavy cavalry, at the same time destroying the invincibility of their castles. The knights had become superfluous through the progress of industry, just as the artisans had become obviated by the same progress. The dire need of the knighthood for money added considerably to their ruin. The luxurious life in the castles, the competition in magnificence at tournaments and feasts, the price of armaments and of horses all increased with the progress of civilisation, whereas the sources of income of the knights and barons, increased but little, if at all. Feuds with accompanying plunders and incendiarism, lying in ambush, and similar noble occupations, became in the course of time too dangerous. The cash payments of the knights' subjects brought in hardly more than before. In order to satisfy mounting requirements, the noble masters resorted to the same means as were practised by the princes; the peasantry was being robbed by the masters with greater dexterity every year. The serfs were being wrung dry. The bondsmen were burdened with ever new payments of various descriptions upon every possible occasion. Serf labour, dues, ground rents, land sale taxes, death taxes, protection moneys and so on, were increased at will in spite of old agreements. Justice was denied or sold for money, and wherever the knight could not obtain the peasant's money otherwise, he threw him into the tower without much ado, and compelled him to pay ransom.

With the other classes, the lower nobility courted no friendly relations either. Vassal knights strove to become vassals of the empire; vassals of the empire strove to become independent. This led to incessant conflicts with the princes. The knighthood looked upon the clergy with their resplendent grandeur as upon a powerful but superfluous class. It envied them their large estates and their riches held secure by celibacy and the church constitution. With the cities, the knighthood was continually on the war path; it owed them money, it fed on plundering their territory, on robbing their merchants, on the ransom paid for prisoners captured in conflicts. The struggle of the knighthood

against all these estates became more vehement as the
estates themselves began to realise that the money question
was a life problem for them.

The clergy, representatives of the ideology of mediæval
feudalism, felt the influence of the historic transformation
no less acutely. The invention of the art of printing, and
the requirements of extended commerce, robbed the clergy
not only of its monopoly of reading and writing, but also
of that of higher education. Division of labour was being
introduced also into the realm of intellectual work. The
newly arising class of jurists drove the clergy out of a
series of very influential positions. The clergy was also
beginning to become largely superfluous, and it acknowl-
edged this fact by growing lazier and more ignorant. The
more superfluous it became, the more it grew in numbers,
thanks to the enormous riches which it still kept on aug-
menting by fair means or foul.

The clergy was divided into two distinct groups. The
feudal hierarchy of the clergy formed the aristocratic group
—bishops and archbishops, abbots, priors and other prelates. These high church dignitaries were either imperial
princes themselves, or they reigned as vassals of other
princes over large areas with numerous serfs and bondsmen.
They not only exploited their subjects as recklessly as the
knighthood and the princes, but they practised this in an
even more shameful manner. They used not only brutal
force, but all the intrigues of religion as well; not only the
horrors of the rack, but also the horror of excommunica-
tion, or refusal of absolution; they used all the intricacies
of the confessional in order to extract from their subjects
the last penny, or to increase the estates of the church.
Forging of documents was a widespread and beloved means
of extortion in the hands of those worthy men, who, re-

ceiving from their subjects feudal payments, taxes and tithes, were still in constant need of money. The manufacture of miracle-producing saints' effigies and relics, the organisation of praying-centres endowed with the power of salvation, the trade in indulgences was resorted to in order to squeeze more payments out of the people. All this was practised long and with not little success.

The prelates and their numerous gendarmerie of monks which grew with the spread of political and religious baiting, were the objects of hatred not only of the people but also of the nobility. Being directly under the empire, the prelates were in the way of the princes. The fast living of the corpulent bishops and abbots with their army of monks, roused the envy of the nobility and the indignation of the people who bore the burden. Hatred was intensified by the fact that the behaviour of the clergy was a slap in the face of their own preaching.

The plebeian faction of the clergy consisted of preachers, rural and urban. The preachers were outside the feudal hierarchy of the church and participated in none of its riches. Their activities were less rigorously controlled and, important as they were for the church, they were for the moment far less indispensable than the police services of the barracked monks. Consequently, they were paid much less than the monks, and their prebends were far from lucrative. Being of a middle-class or plebeian origin, they were nearer to the life of the masses, thus being able to retain middle-class and plebeian sympathies, in spite of their status as clergy. While the participation of the monks in the movements of their time was the exception, that of the plebeian clergy was the rule. They gave the movement its theorists and ideologists, and many of them, representatives of the plebeians and peasants, died on the scaf·

fold. The hatred of the masses for the clergy seldom touched this group.

What the emperor was to the princes and nobility, the pope was to the higher and lower clergy. As the emperor received the "common penny," the imperial taxes, so the pope was paid the general church taxes, out of which he defrayed the expenses of the luxurious Roman court. In no country were his taxes collected with such conscientiousness and rigour as in Germany, due to the power and the number of the clergy. The annates were collected with particular severity when a bishopric was to become vacant. With the growth of the court's demands, new means for raising revenues were invented, such as the traffic in relics and indulgences, jubilee collections, etc. Large sums of money were thus yearly transported from Germany to Rome, and the increased pressure fanned not only the hatred towards the clergy, but it also aroused national feelings, particularly among the nobility, the then most national class.

In the cities, the growth of commerce and handicraft produced three distinct groups out of the original citizenry of mediæval times.

The city population was headed by the *patrician families,* the so-called "honourables." Those were the richest families. They alone sat in the council, and held all the city offices. They not only administered all the revenues of the city, but they also consumed them. Strong in their riches and their ancient aristocratic status, recognised by emperor and empire, they exploited in every possible way the city community as well as the peasants belonging to the city. They practised usury in grain and money; they secured for themselves monopolies of various kinds; they gradually deprived the community of every right to use the city forests and meadows, and used them directly for their own private benefit. They imposed road, bridge and gate payments and other duties; they sold trade and guild privileges, master and citizen rights; and they traded with justice. The peasants of the city area were treated by them with no more consideration than by the nobility and the clergy. On the contrary, the city magistrates and bailiffs, mostly patricians, brought into the villages, together with aristocratic rigidity and avarice, a certain bureaucratic punctuality in collecting duties. The city revenues thus collected were administered in a most optional fashion; city bookkeeping was as neglectful and confused as possible; defraudation and treasury deficits were the order of the day. How easy it was for a comparatively small caste, surrounded by privileges, and held together by family ties and community of interests, to enrich itself enormously out of the city revenues, will be understood when one considers the numerous frauds and swindles which 1848 witnessed in many city administrations.

The patricians took care to make dormant the rights of the city community everywhere, particularly as regards finance. Later, when the extortions of these gentlemen became too severe, the communities started a movement to bring at least the city administration under their control. In most cities they actually regained their rights, but due, on the one hand, to the eternal squabbles between the guilds and, on the other, to the tenacity of the patricians and their protection by the empire and the governments of the allied cities, the patrician council members soon restored by shrewdness or force their dominance in the councils. At the beginning of the Sixteenth Century, the communities of all the cities were again in the opposition.

The city opposition against the patricians was divided

into two factions which stood out very clearly in the course of the peasant war.

The *middle-class opposition*, the predecessor of our modern liberals, embraced the richer middle-class, the middle-class of moderate means, and a more or less appreciable section of the poorer elements, according to local conditions. This opposition demanded control over the city administration and participation in the legislative power either through a general assemblage of the community or through representatives (big council, city committee). Further, it demanded modification of the patrician policy of favouring a few families which were gaining an exceptional position inside the patrician group. Aside from this, the middle-class opposition demanded the filling of some council offices by citizens of their own group. This party, joined here and there by dissatisfied elements of impoverished patricians, had a large majority in all the ordinary general assemblies of the community and in the guilds. The adherents of the council and the more radical opposition formed together only a minority among the real citizens.

We shall see how, in the course of the Sixteenth Century, this moderate, "law-abiding," well-off and intelligent opposition played exactly the same rôle and exactly with the same success as its heir, the constitutional party in the movements of 1848 and 1849. The middle-class opposition had still another object of heated protest: the clergy, whose loose way of living and luxurious habits aroused its bitter scorn. The middle-class opposition demanded measures against the scandalous behaviour of those illustrious people. It demanded that the inner jurisdiction of the clergy and its right to levy taxes should be abolished, and that the number of the monks should be limited.

The *plebeian opposition* consisted of ruined members of the middle-class and that mass of the city population which possessed no citizenship rights: the journeymen, the day labourers, and the numerous beginnings of the *lumpenproletariat* which can be found even in the lowest stages of development of city life. This low-grade proletariat is, generally speaking, a phenomenon which, in a more or less developed form, can be found in all the phases of society hitherto observed. The number of people without a definite occupation and a stable domicile was at that time gradually being augmented by the decay of feudalism in a society in which every occupation, every realm of life, was intrenched behind a number of privileges. In no modern country was the number of vagabonds so great as in Germany, in the first half of the Sixteenth Century. One portion of these tramps joined the army in war-time, another begged its way through the country, a third sought to eke out a meagre living as day-labourers in those branches of work which were not under guild jurisdiction. All three groups played a rôle in the peasant war; the first in the army of the princes to whom the peasant succumbed, the second in the conspiracies and in the troops of the peasants where its demoralising influence was manifested every moment; the third, in the struggles of the parties in the cities. It must be borne in mind, however, that a large portion of this class, namely, the one living in the cities, still retained a considerable foundation of peasant nature, and had not developed that degree of venality and degradation which characterise the modern civilised low-grade proletariat.

It is evident that the plebeian opposition of the cities was of a mixed nature. It combined the ruined elements of the old feudal and guild societies with the budding proletarian elements of a coming modern bourgeois society; on the one hand, impoverished guild citizens, who, due to their privileges, still clung to the existing middle-class order, on the other hand, driven out peasants and ex-officers who were yet unable to become proletarians. Between these two groups were the journeymen, for the time being outside official society and so close to the standard of living of the proletariat as was possible under the industry of the times and the guild privileges, but, due to the same privileges, almost all prospective middle-class master artisans. The party affiliations of this mixture were, naturally, highly uncertain, and varying from locality to locality. Before the peasant war, the plebeian opposition appeared in the political struggles, not as a party, but as a shouting, rapacious tail-end to the middle-class opposition, a mob that could be bought and sold for a few barrels of wine. It was the revolt of the peasants that transformed them into a party, and even then they were almost everywhere dependent upon the peasants, both in demands and in action, —a striking proof of the fact that the cities of that time were greatly dependent upon the country. In so far as the plebeian opposition acted independently, it demanded extension of city trade privileges over the rural districts, and it did like to see the city revenues curtailed by abolition of feudal burdens in the rural area belonging to the city, etc. In brief, in so far as it appeared independently, it was reactionary. It submitted to its own middle-class elements, and thus formed a characteristic prologue to the tragic comedy staged by the modern petty-bourgeoisie in the last three years under the head of democracy.

Only in Thuringia and in a few other localities was the plebeian faction of the city carried away by the general storm to such an extent that its embryo proletarian elements for a brief time gained the upper hand over all the other factors of the movement. This took place under the direct influence of Muenzer in Thuringia, and of his disciples in other places. This episode, forming the climax of the entire peasant war, and grouped around the magnificent figure of Thomas Muenzer, was of very brief duration. It is easily understood why these elements collapse more quickly than any other, why their movement bears an outspoken, fantastic stamp, and why the expression of their demands must necessarily be extremely indefinite. It was this group that found least firm ground in the then existing conditions.

At the bottom of all the classes, save the last one, was the huge exploited mass of the nation, *the peasants*. It was the peasant who carried the burden of all the other strata of society: princes, officialdom, nobility, clergy, patricians and middle-class. Whether the peasant was the subject of a prince, an imperial baron, a bishop, a monastery or a city, he was everywhere treated as a beast of burden, and worse. If he was a serf, he was entirely at the mercy of his master. If he was a bondsman, the legal deliveries stipulated by agreement were sufficient to crush him; even they were being daily increased. Most of his time, he had to work on his master's estate. Out of that which he earned in his few free hours, he had to pay tithes, dues, ground rents, war taxes, land taxes, imperial taxes, and other payments. He could neither marry nor die without paying the master. Aside from his regular work for the master, he had to gather litter, pick strawberries, pick bilberries, collect snail-shells, drive the game for the hunting, chop wood, and so on. Fishing and hunting belonged to the master. The peasant saw his crop destroyed by wild game. The community meadows and woods of the peasants had almost everywhere been forcibly taken away by the masters. And in the same manner as the master reigned over the peasant's property, he extended his wilfulness over

his person, his wife and daughters. He possessed the right
of the first night. Whenever he pleased, he threw the
peasant into the tower, where the rack waited for him
just as surely as the investigating attorney waits for the
criminal in our times. Whenever he pleased, he killed him
or ordered him beheaded. None of the instructive chapters
of the Carolina [3] which speaks of "cutting of ears," "cutting
of noses," "blinding," "chopping of fingers," "beheading,"
"breaking on the wheel," "burning," "pinching with burning tongs," "quartering," etc., was left unpractised by the
gracious lord and master at his pleasure. Who could defend the peasant? The courts were manned by barons,
clergymen, patricians, or jurists, who knew very well for
what they were being paid. Not in vain did all the official
estates of the empire live on the exploitation of the peasants.

Incensed as were the peasants under terrific pressure, it
was still difficult to arouse them to revolt. Being spread
over large areas, it was highly difficult for them to come to
a common understanding; the old habit of submission inherited from generation to generation, the lack of practise
in the use of arms in many regions, the unequal degree of exploitation depending on the personality of the master, all
combined to keep the peasant quiet. It is for these reasons
that, although local insurrections of peasants can be found
in mediæval times in large numbers, not one general national peasant revolt, least of all in Germany, can be observed before the peasant war. Moreover, the peasants
alone could never make a revolution as long as they were
confronted by the organised power of the princes, nobility
and the cities. Only by allying themselves with other
classes could they have a chance of victory, but how could
they have allied themselves with other classes when they
were equally exploited by all?

At the beginning of the Sixteenth Century the various groups of the empire, princes, nobility, clergy, patricians, middle-class, plebeians and peasants formed a highly complicated mass with the most varied requirements crossing each other in different directions. Every group was in the way of the other, and stood continually in an overt or covert struggle with every other group. A splitting of the entire nation into two major camps, as witnessed in France at the outbreak of the first revolution, and as at present manifest on a higher stage of development in the most progressive countries, was under such conditions a rank impossibility. Something approaching such division took place only when the lowest stratum of the population, the one exploited by all the rest, arose, namely, the plebeians and the peasants. The tangle of interests, views and endeavours of that time will be easily understood when one remembers what a confusion was manifested in the last two years in a society far less complicated and consisting only of feudal nobility, bourgeoisie, petty-bourgeoisie, peasants and proletariat.

CHAPTER II

THE grouping of the numerous and variegated groups into bigger units was at that time made impossible by decentralisation, by local and provincial independence, by industrial and commercial isolation of the provinces from each other, and by poor means of communication. This grouping develops only with the general spread of revolutionary, religious and political ideas, in the course of the Reformation. The various groups of the population which either accept or oppose those ideas, concentrate the nation, very slowly and only approximately indeed, into three large camps, the reactionary or Catholic, the reformist middle-class or Lutheran, and the revolutionary elements. If we discover little logic even in this great division of the nation, if the first two camps include partly the same elements, it is due to the fact that most of the official groupings brought over from the Middle Ages had begun to dissolve and to become decentralised, which circumstance gave to the same groups in different localities a momentary opposing orientation. In the last years we have so often met with similar facts in Germany that we will not be surprised at this apparent mixture of groups and classes under the much more complicated conditions of the Sixteenth Century.

The German ideology of to-day sees in the struggles to which the Middle Ages had succumbed nothing but violent theological bickerings, this notwithstanding our modern experiences. Had the people of that time only been able to reach an understanding concerning the celestial things, say our patriotic historians and wise statesmen, there would have been no ground whatever for struggle over earthly affairs. These ideologists were gullible enough to accept on their face value all the illusions which an epoch maintains about itself, or which the ideologists of a certain period maintained about that period. This class of people, which saw in the revolution of 1789 nothing but a heated debate over the advantages of a constitutional monarchy as compared with absolutism, would see in the July Revolution a practical controversy over the untenability of the empire by the grace of God, and in the February Revolution, an attempt at solving the problem of a republic or monarchy, etc. Of the *class struggles* which were being fought out in these convulsions, and whose mere expression is being every time written as a political slogan on the banner of these class struggles, our ideologists have no conception even at the present time, although manifestations of them are audible enough not only abroad, but also from the grumbling and the resentment of many thousands of home proletarians.

In the so-called religious wars of the Sixteenth Century, very positive material class-interests were at play, and those wars were class wars just as were the later collisions in England and France. If the class struggles of that time appear to bear religious earmarks, if the interests, requirements and demands of the various classes hid themselves behind a religious screen, it little changes the actual situation, and is to be explained by conditions of the time.

The Middle Ages had developed out of raw primitiveness. It had done away with old civilisation, old philosophy, politics and jurisprudence, in order to begin anew in every respect. The only thing which it had retained from the old shattered world was Christianity and a number of half-

ruined cities deprived of their civilisation. As a consequence, the clergy retained a monopoly of intellectual education, a phenomenon to be found in every primitive stage
of development, and education itself had acquired a predominantly theological nature.

In the hands of the clergy, politics and jurisprudence, as
well as other sciences, remained branches of theology, and
were treated according to the principles prevailing in the
latter. The dogmas of the church were at the same time
political axioms, and Bible quotations had the validity of
law in every court. Even after the formation of a special class of jurists, jurisprudence long remained under the
tutelage of theology. This supremacy of theology in the
realm of intellectual activities was at the same time a logical
consequence of the situation of the church as the most
general force co-ordinating and sanctioning existing feudal
domination.

It is obvious that under such conditions, all general and
overt attacks on feudalism, in the first place attacks on the
church, all revolutionary, social and political doctrines,
necessarily became theological heresies. In order to be
attacked, existing social conditions had to be stripped of
their aureole of sanctity.

The revolutionary opposition to feudalism was alive
throughout all the Middle Ages. According to conditions
of the time, it appeared either in the form of mysticism, as
open heresy, or of armed insurrection. As mysticism, it is
well known how indispensable it was for the reformers of
the Sixteenth Century. Muenzer himself was largely in-
debted to it. The heresies were partly an expression of the
reaction of the patriarchal Alpine shepherds against the en-
croachments of feudalism in their realm (Waldenses),[4]
partly an opposition to feudalism of the cities that had out-

grown it (The Albigenses, Arnold of Brescia, etc.), and partly direct insurrections of peasants (John Ball, the master from Hungary in Picardy, etc.). We can omit, in this connection, the patriarchal heresy of the Waldenses, as well as the insurrection of the Swiss, which by form and contents, was a reactionary attempt at stemming the tide of historic development, and of a purely local importance. In the other two forms of mediæval heresy, we find as early as the Twelfth Century the precursors of the great division between the middle-class and the peasant-plebeian opposition which caused the collapse of the peasant war. This division is manifest throughout the later Middle Ages.

The heresy of the cities, which is the actual official heresy of the Middle Ages, directed itself primarily against the clergy, whose riches and political importance it attacked. In the very same manner as the bourgeoisie at present demands a *"gouvernement à bon marché"* (cheap government), so the middle-class of mediæval times demanded first of all an *"église à bon marché"* (cheap church). Reactionary in form, as is every heresy which sees in the further development of church and dogma only a degeneration, the middle-class heresy demanded the restoration of the ancient simple church constitution and the abolition of an exclusive class of priests. This cheap arrangement would eliminate the monks, the prelates, the Roman court, in brief, everything which was expensive for the church. In their attack against papacy, the cities, themselves republics although under the protection of monarchs, expressed for the first time in a general form the idea that the normal form of government for the bourgeoisie was the republic. Their hostility towards many a dogma and church law is partly explained by the foregoing and partly by their conditions. Why they were so bitter against celibacy, no one has given a better explanation than Boccaccio. Arnold of Brescia [5] in Italy and Germany, the Albigenses [6] in south France, John Wycliffe [7] in England, Huss [8] and the Calixtines [9] in Bohemia, were the chief representatives of this opposition. That the opposition against feudalism should appear here only as an opposition against religious feudalism, is easily understood when one remembers that, at that time, the cities were already a recognised estate sufficiently capable of fighting lay feudalism with its privileges either by force of arms or in the city assemblies.

Here, as in south France, in England and Bohemia, we find the lower nobility joining hands with the cities in their struggle against the clergy and in their heresies, a phenomenon due to the dependence of the lower nobility upon the cities and to the community of interests of both groups as against the princes and the prelates. The same phenomenon is found in the peasant war.

A totally different character was assumed by that heresy which was a direct expression of the peasant and plebeian demands, and which was almost always connected with an insurrection. This heresy, sharing all the demands of middle-class heresy relative to the clergy, the papacy, and the restoration of the ancient Christian church organisation, went far beyond them. It demanded the restoration of ancient Christian equality among the members of the community, this to be recognised as a rule for the middle-class world as well. From the equality of the children of God it made the implication as to civil equality, and partly also as to equality of property. To make the nobility equal to the peasant, the patricians and the privileged middle-class equal to the plebeians, to abolish serfdom, ground rents, taxes, privileges, and at least the most flagrant differences of property—these were demands put forth with more or less definiteness and regarded as naturally emanat٠ ing from the ancient Christian doctrine. This peasant-plebeian heresy, in the fullness of feudalism, e. g., among the Albigenses, hardly distinguishable from the middle-class opposition, grew in the course of the Fourteenth and Fifteenth Centuries to be a strongly defined party opinion appearing independently alongside the heresy of the middle-class. This is the case with John Ball, preacher of the Wat Tyler insurrection in England alongside the Wycliffe movement. This is also the case with the Taborites[9] alongside the Calixtines in Bohemia. The Taborites showed even a republican tendency under theocratic colouring, a view later developed by the representatives of the plebeians in Germany in the Fifteenth and at the beginning of the Sixteenth Century.

This form of heresy was joined in by the dream visions of the mystic sects, such as the Scourging Friars,[10] the Lollards,[11] etc., which in times of suppression continued revolutionary tradition.

The plebeians of that time were the only class outside of the existing official society. It was outside the feudal, as well as outside the middle-class organisation. It had neither privileges nor property; it was deprived even of the possessions owned by peasant or petty bourgeois, burdened with crushing duties as much as they might be; it was deprived of property and rights in every respect; it lived in such a manner that it did not even come into direct contact with the existing institutions, which ignored it completely. It was a living symptom of the dissolution of the feudal and guild middle-class societies, and it was at the same time the first precursor of modern bourgeois society.

This position of the plebeians is sufficient explanation as to why the plebeian opposition of that time could not be satisfied with fighting feudalism and the privileged middle-class alone; why, in fantasy, at least, it reached beyond modern bourgeois society then only in its inception; why, being an absolutely propertyless faction, it questioned institutions, views and conceptions common to every society based on division of classes. The chiliastic dream-visions [12] of ancient Christianity offered in this respect a very serviceable starting-point. On the other hand, this reaching out beyond not only the present but also the future, could not help being violently fantastic. At the first practical application, it naturally fell back into narrow limits set by prevailing conditions. The attack on private property, the demand for community of possession had to solve itself into a crude organisation of charity; vague Christian equality could result in nothing but civic equality before the law; abolition of all officialdom transformed itself finally in the organisation of republican governments elected by the people. Anticipation of communism by human fantasy was in reality anticipation of modern bourgeois conditions.

This anticipation of coming stages of historic development, forced in itself, but a natural outcome of the life conditions of the plebeian group, is first to be noted in Germany, in the teachings of Thomas Muenzer and his party. Already the Taborites showed a kind of chiliastic community of property, but this was a purely military measure. Only in the teachings of Muenzer did these communist notions find expression as the desires of a vital section of society. Through him they were formulated with a certain definiteness, and were afterwards found in every great convulsion of the people, until gradually they merged with the modern proletarian movement. Something similar we observe in the Middle Ages, where the struggles of the free peasants against increasing feudal domination merged with the struggles of the serfs and bondsmen for the complete abolition of the feudal system.

While the first of the three large camps, the conservative Catholics, embraced all the elements interested in maintaining the existing imperial power, the ecclesiastical and a section of the lay princes, the richer nobility, the prelates and the city patricians—the middle-class moderate Lutheran reform gathered under its banner all the propertied elements of the opposition, the mass of the lower nobility, the middle-class and even a portion of the lay princes who hoped to enrich themselves through the confiscation of the church estates and to seize the opportunity for establishing greater independence from the empire. As to the peasants and plebeians, they grouped themselves around the revolutionary party whose demands and doctrines found their boldest expression in Muenzer.

Luther [13] and Muenzer, in their doctrines, in their characters, in their actions, accurately embodied the tenets of their separate parties.

Between 1517 and 1525, Luther had gone through the same transformations as the German constitutionalists between 1846 and 1849. This has been the case with every middle-class party which, having marched for a while at the head of the movement, has been overwhelmed by the plebeian-proletarian party pressing from the rear.

When in 1517 opposition against the dogmas and the organisation of the Catholic church was first raised by Luther, it still had no definite character. Not exceeding the demands of the earlier middle-class heresy, it did not exclude any trend of opinion which went further. It could not do so because the first moment of the struggle demanded that all opposing elements be united, the most aggressive revolutionary energy be utilised, and the totality of the

existing heresies fighting the Catholic orthodoxy be represented. In a similar fashion, our liberal bourgeoisie of 1847
were still revolutionary. They called themselves socialists
and communists, and they discussed emancipation of the
working class. Luther's sturdy peasant nature asserted
itself in the stormiest fashion in the first period of his
activities. "If the raging madness [of the Roman church-
men] were to continue, it seems to me no better counsel
and remedy could be found against it than that kings and
princes apply force, arm themselves, attack those evil people
who have poisoned the entire world, and once and for all
make an end to this game, *with arms, not with words.* If
thieves are being punished with swords, murderers with
ropes, and heretics with fire, why do we not seize, with
arms in hand, all those evil teachers of perdition, those
popes, bishops, cardinals, and the entire crew of Roman
Sodom? Why do we not wash our hands in their blood?"

This revolutionary ardour did not last long. The lightning thrust by Luther caused a conflagration. A movement
started among the entire German people. In his appeals
against the clergy, in his preaching of Christian freedom,
peasants and plebeians perceived the signal for insurrection.
Likewise, the moderate middle-class and a large section of
the lower nobility joined him, and even princes were drawn
into the torrent. While the former believed the day had
come in which to wreak vengeance upon all their oppressors,
the latter only wished to break the power of the clergy, the
dependence upon Rome, the Catholic hierarchy, and to enrich themselves through the confiscation of church property.
The parties became separated from each other, and each
found a different spokesman. Luther had to choose between
the two. Luther, the protégé of the Elector of Saxony, the
respected professor of Wittenberg who had become powerful

and famous overnight, the great man who was surrounded by a coterie of servile creatures and flatterers, did not hesitate a moment. He dropped the popular elements of the movement, and joined the train of the middle-class, the nobility and the princes. Appeals to a war of extermination against Rome were heard no more. Luther was now preaching *peaceful progress* and passive resistance. (Cf. *To the nobility of the German nation*, 1520, etc.) Invited by Hutten to visit him and Sickingen in the castle of Ebern, the centre of the noble conspiracy against clergy and princes, Luther replied: *"I should not like to see the Gospel defended by force and bloodshed.* The world was conquered by the Word, the Church has maintained itself by the Word, the Church will come into its own again through the Word, and as Antichrist gained ascendency without violence, so without violence he will fall."

Out of this turn of mind, or, to be more exact, out of this definite delineation of Luther's policy, sprang that policy of bartering and haggling over institutions and dogmas to be retained or reformed, that ugly diplomatising, conceding, intriguing and compromising, the result of which was the Augsburg Confession,[13] the final draft of the constitution of the reformed middle-class church. It was the same petty trading which, in the political field, repeated itself *ad nauseam* in the recent German national assemblies, unity gatherings, chambers of revision, and in the parliaments of Erfurt. The Philistine middle-class character of the official reformation appeared in these negotiations most clearly.

There were valid reasons why Luther, now the recognised representative of middle-class reform, chose to preach lawful progress. The mass of the cities had joined the cause of moderate reform; the lower nobility became more and more devoted to it; one section of the princes joined it, another vacillated. Success was almost certain at least in a large portion of Germany. Under continued peaceful development the other regions could not in the long run withstand the pressure of moderate opposition. Violent convulsions, on the other hand, were bound to result in a conflict between the moderates and the extreme plebeian and peasant party, thus to alienate the princes, the nobility, and a number of cities from the movement and to leave open the alternative of either the middle-class party being overshadowed by the peasants and plebeians, or the entire movement being crushed by Catholic restoration. How middle-class parties, having achieved the slightest victory, attempt to steer their way between the Scylla of revolution and the Charybdis of restoration by means of lawful progress, we have had occasions enough to observe in the events of recent times.

It was in the nature of the then prevailing social and political conditions that the results of every change were advantageous to the princes, increasing their power. Thus it came about that the middle-class reform, having parted ways with the plebeian and peasant elements, fell more and more under the control of the reform princes. Luther's subservience to them increased, and the people knew very well what they were doing when they accused him of having become a slave of the princes as were all the others, and when they pursued him with stones in Orlamuende.

When the peasant war broke out, becoming more predominant in regions with Catholic nobility and princes, Luther strove to maintain a conciliatory position. He resolutely attacked the governments. He said it was due to their oppression that the revolts had started, that not the peasants alone were against them, but God as well. On the other hand, he also said that the revolt was ungodly and against the Gospel. He advised both parties to yield, to reach a peaceful understanding.

Notwithstanding these sincere attempts at conciliation, however, the revolt spread rapidly over large areas, including such sections as were dominated by Protestant Lutheran princes, nobles and cities, and rapidly outgrew the middle-class "circumspect" reform. The most determined faction of the insurgents under Muenzer opened their headquarters in Luther's very proximity, in Thuringia. A few more successes, and Germany would have been one big conflagration, Luther would have been surrounded, perhaps piked as a traitor, and middle-class reform would have been swept away by the tides of a peasant-plebeian revolution. There was no more time for circumspection. In the face of the revolution, all old animosities were forgotten. Compared with the hordes of peasants, the servants of the Roman Sodom were innocent lambs, sweet-tempered children of God. Burgher and prince, noble and clergyman, Luther and the pope united "against the murderous and plundering hordes of the peasants." "They should be knocked to pieces, strangled and stabbed, secretly and openly, by everybody who can do it, just as one must kill a mad dog!" Luther cried. "Therefore, dear gentlemen, hearken here, save there, stab, knock, strangle them at will, and if thou diest, thou art blessed; no better death canst thou ever attain." No false mercy was to be practised in relation to the peasants. "Whoever hath pity on those whom God pities not, whom He wishes punished and destroyed, shall be classed among the rebellious himself." Later, he said, the peasants would learn to thank God when they had to give away one cow in order that they might enjoy the other in peace. Through the revolution, he said, the princes would learn the spirit of the mob which could reign by force only. "The wise man says: '*Cibus, onus et virgam asino.*' The heads of the peasants are full of chaff. They do not hearken to the Word, and they are senseless, so they must hearken to the virga and the gun, and this is only just. We must pray for them that they obey. Where they do not, there should not be much mercy. Let the guns roar among them, or else they will make it a thousand times worse."

It is the same language that was used by our late socialist and philanthropic bourgeoisie, when, after the March days the proletariat also demanded its share in the fruits of victory.

Luther had given the plebeian movement a powerful weapon—a translation of the Bible. Through the Bible, he contrasted feudal Christianity of his time with moderate Christianity of the first century. In opposition to decaying feudal society, he held up the picture of another society which knew nothing of the ramified and artificial feudal hierarchy. The peasants had made extensive use of this weapon against the forces of the princes, the nobility, and the clergy. Now Luther turned the same weapon against the peasants, extracting from the Bible a veritable hymn to the authorities ordained by God—a feat hardly exceeded by any lackey of absolute monarchy. Princedom by the grace of God, passive resistance, even serfdom, were being sanctioned by the Bible. Thus Luther repudiated not only the peasant insurrection but even his own revolt against religious and lay authority. He not only betrayed the popular movement to the princes, but the middle-class movement as well.

Need we mention other bourgeois who recently gave us examples of repudiating their own past?

Let us now compare the plebeian revolutionary, Muenzer, with the middle-class reformist, Luther.

Thomas Muenzer was born in Stolberg, in the Harz, in 1498. It is said that his father died on the scaffold, a victim of the wilfulness of the Count of Stolberg. In his fifteenth year, Muenzer organised at the Halle school a secret union against the Archbishop of Magdeburg and the Roman Church in general. His scholarly attainments in the theology of his time brought him early the doctor's degree and the position of chaplain in a Halle nunnery. Here he began to treat the dogmas and rites of the church with the greatest contempt. At mass he omitted the words of the transubstantiation, and ate, as Luther said, the almighty gods unconsecrated. Mediæval mystics, especially the chiliastic works of Joachim of Calabria,[14] were the main subject of his studies. It seemed to Muenzer that the millennium and the day of judgment over the degenerated church and the corrupted world, as announced and pictured by that mystic, had come in the form of the Reformation and the general restlessness of his time. He preached in his neighbourhood with great success. In 1520 he went to Zwickau as the first evangelist preacher. There he found one of those dreamy chiliastic sects which continued their existence in many localities, hiding behind an appearance of humility and detachment, the rankly growing opposition of the lower strata of society against existing conditions, and with the growth of agitation, beginning to press to the foreground more boldly and with more endurance. It was the sect of the Anabaptists headed by Nicolas Storch.[15] The Anabaptists preached the approach of the Day of Judgment and of the millennium; they had "visions, convulsions, and the spirit of prophecy." They soon came into conflict with the council of Zwickau. Muenzer defended them, though he had never joined them unconditionally, and had rather brought them under his own influence. The council took decisive steps against them, they were compelled to leave the city, and Muenzer departed with them. This was at the end of 1521.

He then went to Prague and, in order to gain ground, attempted to join the remnants of the Hussite movement. His proclamations, however, made it necessary for him to flee Bohemia also. In 1522, he became preacher at Altstedt in Thuringia. Here he started with reforming the cult. Before even Luther dared to go so far, he entirely abolished the Latin language, and ordered the entire Bible, not only the prescribed Sunday Gospels and epistles, to be read to the people. At the same time, he organised propaganda in his locality. People flocked to him from all directions, and soon Altstedt became the centre of the popular anti-priest movement of entire Thuringia.

Muenzer at that time was still theologian before everything else. He directed his attacks almost exclusively against the priests. He did not, however, preach quiet debate and peaceful progress, as Luther had begun to do at that time, but he continued the early violent preachments of Luther, appealing to the princes of Saxony and the people to rise in arms against the Roman priests. "Is it not Christ who said: 'I have come to bring, not peace, but the sword'? What can you [the princes of Saxony] do with that sword? You can do only one thing: If you wish to be the servants of God, you must drive out and destroy the evil ones who stand in the way of the Gospel. Christ ordered very earnestly (Luke, 19, 27): 'But these mine enemies, that would not that I should reign over them, bring hither, and slay them before me.' Do not resort to empty assertions that the power of God could do it without aid of our sword, since then it would have to rust in its sheath. We must destroy those who stand in the way of God's revelation, we mus' do it mercilessly, as Hezekiah, Cyrus, Josiah, Daniel and Elias destroyed the priests of Baal, else the Christian Church will never come back to its origins. We must uproot the weeds in God's vineyard at the time when the crops are ripe. God said in the Fifth Book of Moses, 7, 'Thou shalt not show mercy unto the idolators, but ye shall break down their altars, dash in pieces their graven images and burn them with fire that I shall not be wroth at you.'"

But these appeals to the princes were of no avail, whereas the revolutionary agitation among the people grew day by day. Muenzer, whose ideas became more definitely shaped and more courageous, now definitely relinquished the middle-class reformation, and at the same time appeared as a direct political agitator.

His theologic-philosophic doctrine attacked all the main points not only of Catholicism but of Christianity as such. Under the cloak of Christian forms, he preached a kind of pantheism, which curiously resembles the modern speculative mode of contemplation, and at times even taught open atheism. He repudiated the assertion that the Bible was the only infallible revelation. The only living revelation, he said, was reason, a revelation which existed among all peoples at all times. To contrast the Bible with reason, he maintained, was to kill the spirit by the latter, for the Holy Spirit of which the Bible spoke was not a thing outside of us; the Holy Spirit was our reason. Faith, he said, was nothing else but reason become alive in man, therefore, he said, pagans could also have faith. Through this faith, through reason come to life, man became godlike and blessed, he said. Heaven was to be sought in this life, not beyond, and it was, according to Muenzer, the task of the

believers to establish Heaven, the kingdom of God, here
on earth. As there is no Heaven in the beyond, he asserted,
so there is no Hell in the beyond, and no damnation, and
there are no devils but the evil desires and cravings of man.
Christ, he said, was a man, as we are, a prophet and a
teacher, and his "Lord's Supper" is nothing but a plain
meal of commemoration wherein bread and wine are being
consumed with mystic additions.

Muenzer preached these doctrines mostly in a covert
fashion, under the cloak of Christian phraseology which the
new philosophy was compelled to utilise for some time.
The fundamental heretic idea, however, is easily discernible
in all his writings, and it is obvious that the biblical cloak
was for him of much less importance than it was for many
a disciple of Hegel in modern times. Still, there is a dis-
tance of three hundred years between Muenzer and modern
philosophy.

Muenzer's political doctrine followed his revolutionary
religious conceptions very closely, and as his theology
reached far beyond the current conceptions of his time, so
his political doctrine went beyond existing social and political conditions. As Muenzer's philosophy of religion touched
upon atheism, so his political programme touched upon communism, and there is more than one communist sect of
modern times which, on the eve of the February Revolution, did not possess a theoretical equipment as rich as
that of Muenzer of the Sixteenth Century. His programme,
less a compilation of the demands of the then existing plebeians than a genius's anticipation of the conditions for the
emancipation of the proletarian element that had just begun
to develop among the plebeians, demanded the immediate
establishment of the kingdom of God, of the prophesied
millennium on earth. This was to be accomplished by the

return of the church to its origins and the abolition of all institutions that were in conflict with what Muenzer conceived as original Christianity, which, in fact, was the idea of a very modern church. By the kingdom of God, Muenzer understood nothing else than a state of society without class differences, without private property, and without superimposed state powers opposed to the members of society. All existing authorities, as far as they did not submit and join the revolution, he taught, must be overthrown, all work and all property must be shared in common, and complete equality must be introduced. In his conception, a union of the people was to be organised to realise this programme, not only throughout Germany, but throughout entire Christendom. Princes and nobles were to be invited to join, and should they refuse, the union was to overthrow or kill them, with arms in hand, at the first opportunity.

Muenzer immediately set to work to organise the union. His preachings assumed a still more militant character. He attacked, not only the clergy, but with equal passion the princes, the nobility and the patricians. He pictured in burning colours the existing oppression, and contrasted it with the vision of the millennium of social republican equality which he created out of his imagination. He published one revolutionary pamphlet after another, sending emissaries in all directions, while he personally organised the union in Altstedt and its vicinity.

The first fruit of this propaganda was the destruction of St. Mary's Chapel in Mellerbach near Altstedt, according to the command of the Bible (Deut. 7, 5): "Ye shall break down their altars, and dash in pieces their pillars, and hew down their Asherim, and burn their graven images with fire." The princes of Saxony came in person to Altstedt to quell the upheaval, and they called Muenzer to the castle.

There he delivered a sermon, which they had never heard from Luther, "that easy living flesh of Wittenberg," as Muenzer called him. He insisted that the ungodly rulers, especially the priests and monks who treated the Gospel as heresy, must be killed; for confirmation he referred to the New Testament. The ungodly have no right to live, he said, save by the mercy of the chosen ones. If the princes would not exterminate the ungodly, he asserted, God would take their sword from them because the right to wield the sword belongs to the community. The source of the evil of usury, thievery and robbery, he said, were the princes and the masters who had taken all creatures into their private possession—the fishes in the water, the birds in the air, the plants in the soil. And the usurpers, he said, still preached to the poor the commandment, "Thou shalt not steal," while they grabbed everything, and robbed and crushed the peasant and the artisan. "When, however, one of the latter commits the slightest transgression," he said, "he has to hang, and Dr. Liar says to all this: Amen." The masters themselves created a situation, he argued, in which the poor man was forced to become their enemy. If they did not remove the causes of the upheaval, how could things improve in times to come? he asked. "Oh, my dear gentlemen, how the Lord will smite with an iron rod all these old pots! When I say so, I am considered rebellious. So be it!" (Cf. Zimmermann's *Peasant War*, II, p. 75.)

Muenzer had the sermon printed. His Altstedt printer was punished by Duke Johann of Saxony with banishment. His own writings were to be henceforth subjected to the censorship of the ducal government in Weimar. But he paid no heed to this order. He immediately published a very inciting paper in the imperial city of Muehlhausen, wherein he admonished the people "to widen the hole so that all the world may see and comprehend who our fools are who have blasphemously turned our Lord into a painted mannikin." He concluded with the following words: "All the world must suffer a big jolt. The game will be such that the ungodly will be thrown off their seats and the downtrodden will rise." As a motto, Thomas Muenzer, "the man with the hammer," wrote the following on the title page: "Beware, I have put my words into thy mouth; I have lifted thee above the people and above the empires that thou mayest uproot, destroy, scatter and overthrow, and that thou mayest build and plant. A wall of iron against the kings, princes, priests, and for the people hath been erected. Let them fight, for victory is wondrous, and the strong and godless tyrants will perish."

The breach between Muenzer and Luther with his party had taken place long before that. Luther himself was compelled to accept some church reforms which were introduced by Muenzer without consulting him. Luther watched Muenzer's activities with the nettled distrust of a moderate reformer towards an energetic far-aiming radical. Already in the spring of 1524, in a letter to Melanchthon, that model of a hectic stay-at-home Philistine, Muenzer wrote that he and Luther did not understand the movement at all. They were seeking, he said, to choke it by adherence to the letter of the Bible, and their doctrine was worm-eaten. "Dear brethren," he wrote, "stop your delaying and hesitating. The time has come, the summer is knocking at our doors. Do not keep friendship with the ungodly who prevent the Word from exercising its full force. Do not flatter your princes in order that you may not perish with them. Ye tender, bookish scholars, do not be wroth, for I cannot do otherwise."

Luther had more than once invited Muenzer to an open

debate. The latter, however, being always ready to accept battle in the presence of the people, did not have the slightest desire to plunge into a theological squabble before the partisan public of the Wittenberg University. He had no desire "to bring the testimony of the spirit before the high school of learning exclusively." If Luther was sincere, he wrote, let him use his influence to stop the chicaneries against his, Muenzer's, printers, and to lift the censorship in order that their controversy might be freely fought out in the press.

When the above-mentioned revolutionary brochure appeared, Luther openly denounced Muenzer. In his "Letter to the Princes of Saxony Against the Rebellious Spirit," he declared Muenzer to be an instrument of Satan, and demanded of the princes to intervene, and drive the instigators of the upheaval out of the country, since, he said, they did not confine themselves to preaching their evil doctrine, but incited to insurrection, to violent lawless action against the authorities.

On August 1st, Muenzer was compelled to appear before the princes in the castle of Weimar, to defend himself against the accusation of incendiary machinations. There were highly compromising facts quoted against him; his secret union had been traced; his hand was discovered in the organisation of the pitmen and the peasants. He was being threatened with banishment. Upon returning to Altstedt, he learned Duke Georg of Saxony demanded his extradition. Union letters in his handwriting had been intercepted, wherein he called Georg's subjects to armed resistance against the enemies of the Gospel. The council would have extradited him had he not left the city.

In the meantime, the rising agitation among the peasants and the plebeians had enormously lightened Muenzer's task of propaganda. In the person of the Anabaptists he found invaluable agents. This sect, having no definite dogmas, held together by common opposition against all ruling classes and by the common symbol of second baptism, ascetic in their mode of living, untiring, fanatic and intrepid in propaganda, had grouped itself more closely around Muenzer. Made homeless by constant persecutions, its members wandered over the length and breadth of Germany, announcing everywhere the new gospel wherein Muenzer had made clear to them their own demands and wishes. Numberless Anabaptists were put on the rack, burned or otherwise executed. But the courage and endurance of these emissaries were unshaken, and the success of their activities amidst the rapidly rising agitation of the people was enormous. That was one of the reasons why, on his flight from Thuringia, Muenzer found the ground prepared wherever he turned.

In Nuernberg, a peasant revolt had been nipped in the bud a month previous. Here Muenzer conducted his propaganda under cover. Soon there appeared persons who defended his most audacious theological doctrines of the non-obligatory power of the Bible and the meaninglessness of sacraments, declaring Christ to have been a mere man, and the power of lay authorities to be ungodly. "We see there Satan stalking, the spirit of Altstedt!" Luther exclaimed. In Nuernberg, Muenzer printed his reply to Luther. He accused him of flattering the princes and supporting the reactionary party by his moderate position. "The people will free themselves in spite of everything," he wrote, "and then the fate of Dr. Luther will be that of a captive fox." The city council ordered the paper confiscated, and Muenzer was compelled to leave the city. From there he went through Suabia to Alsace, then to Switzerland,

and then back to the Upper Black Forest where the insurrection had started several months before, precipitated largely by the Anabaptist emissaries. There is no doubt that this propaganda trip of Muenzer's added much to the organisation of the people's party, to a clear formulation of its demands and to the final general outbreak of the insurrection in April, 1525. It was through this trip that the dual nature of Muenzer's activities became more and more pronounced—on the one hand, his propaganda among the people whom he approached in the only language then comprehensible to the masses, that of religious prophecy; on the other hand, his contact with the initiated, to whom he could disclose his ultimate aims. Even previous to this journey he had grouped around himself in Thuringia a circle of the most determined persons, not only from among the people, but also from among the lower clergy, a circle whom he had put at the head of the secret organisation. Now he became the centre of the entire revolutionary movement of southwest Germany, organising connections between Saxony and Thuringia through Franconia and Suabia up to Alsace and the Swiss frontier and counting among his disciples and the heads of the organisation such men as Hubmaier of Waldshut, Conrad Grebel of Zurich, Franz Rabmann of Griessen, Schappelar of Memmingen, Jakob Wehe of Leipheim, and Dr. Mantel in Stuttgart, the most revolutionary of priests. He kept himself mostly in Griessen on the Schaffhausen frontier, undertaking journeys through the Hegau, Klettgau, etc. The bloody persecutions undertaken by the alarmed princes and masters everywhere against this new plebeian heresy, aided not a little in fanning the rebellious spirit and closing the ranks of the organisation. In this way, Muenzer passed five months in upper Germany. When the outbreak of the general movement was at hand, he returned to Thuringia, where he wished to lead the movement personally. There we will find him later.

We shall see how truly the character and the behaviour of the two party heads reflected the position of their respective parties. Luther's indecision, his fear of the movement, assumed serious proportions; his cowardly servility towards the princes corresponded closely to the hesitating, vacillating policy of the middle-classes. The revolutionary energy and decisiveness of Muenzer, on the other hand, was seen in the most advanced faction of the plebeians and peasants. The difference was that while Luther confined himself to an expression of the ideas and wishes of a majority of his class and thereby acquired among it a very cheap popularity, Muenzer, on the contrary, went far beyond the immediate ideas and demands of the plebeians and peasants, organising out of the then existing revolutionary elements a party, which, as far as it stood on the level of his ideas and shared his energy, still represented only a small minority of the insurgent masses.

CHAPTER III

ABOUT fifty years after the suppression of the Hussite movement, the first symptoms of a budding revolutionary spirit became manifest among the German peasants.

The first peasant conspiracy came into being in 1476, in the bishopric of Wuerzburg, a country already impoverished "by bad government, manifold taxes, payments, feuds, enmity, war, fires, murders, prison, and the like," and continually plundered by bishops, clergy and nobility in a shameless manner. A young shepherd and musician, Hans Boeheim of Niklashausen, also called the "Drum-Beater" and "Hans the Piper," suddenly appeared in Taubergrund in the rôle of a prophet. He related that the Virgin had appeared to him in a vision, that she told him to burn his drum, to cease serving the dance and the sinful gratification of the senses, and to exhort the people to do penance. Therefore, he said, everybody should purge himself of sin and the vain lusts of the world, forsake all adornments and embellishments, and make a pilgrimage to the Madonna of Niklashausen to attain forgiveness.

Already among these precursors of the movement we notice an asceticism which is to be found in all mediæval uprisings that were tinged with religion, and also in modern times at the beginning of every proletarian movement. This austerity of behaviour, this insistence on relinquishing all enjoyment of life, contrasts the ruling classes with the principle of Spartan equality. Nevertheless, it is a necessary transitional stage, without which the lowest strata of society could never start a movement. In order to develop revolutionary energy, in order to become conscious of their own hostile position towards all other elements of society, in order to concentrate as a class, the lower strata of society must begin with stripping themselves of everything that could reconcile them to the existing system of society. They must renounce all pleasures which would make their subdued position in the least tolerable and of which even the severest pressure could not deprive them.

This plebeian and proletarian asceticism differs widely, both by its wild fanatic form and by its contents, from the middle-class asceticism as preached by the middle-class Lutheran morality and by the English Puritans (to be distinguished from the independent and farther-reaching sects) whose whole secret is middle-class thrift. It is quite obvious that this plebeian-proletarian asceticism loses its revolutionary character when the development of modern productive forces increases the number of commodities, thus rendering Spartan equality superfluous, and on the other hand, the very position of the proletariat in society, and thereby the proletariat itself becomes more and more revolutionary. Gradually, this asceticism disappears from among the masses. Among the sects with which it survives, it degenerates either into bourgeois parsimony or into high-sounding virtuousness which, in the end, is nothing more than Philistine or guild-artisan niggardliness. Besides, renunciation of pleasures need not be preached to the proletariat for the simple reason that it has almost nothing to renounce.

Hans the Piper's call to penitence found a great response. All the prophets of rebellion started with appeals against sin, because, in fact, only a violent exertion, a sudden renunciation of all habitual forms of existence could bring

into unified motion a disunited, widely scattered generation
of peasants grown up in blind submission. A pilgrimage
to Niklashausen began and rapidly increased, and the
greater the masses of people that joined the procession, the
more openly did the young rebel divulge his plans. The
Madonna of Niklashausen, he said, had announced to him
that henceforth there should be neither king nor princes,
neither pope nor other ecclesiastic or lay authority. Every
one should be a brother to each other, and win his bread by
the toil of his hands, possessing no more than his neighbour.
All taxes, ground rents, serf duties, tolls and other payments and deliveries should be abolished forever. Forests,
waters and meadows should be free everywhere.

The people received this new gospel with joy. The fame
of the prophet, "the message of our Mother," spread everywhere, even in distant quarters. Hordes of pilgrims came
from the Odenwald, from Main, from Kocher and Jaxt,
even from Bavaria and Suabia, and from the Rhine. Miracles supposed to have been performed by the Piper were
being related; people fell on their knees before the prophet,
praying to him as to a saint; people fought for small strips
from his cap as for relics or amulets. In vain did the
priests fight him, denouncing his visions as the devil's de-
lusions and his miracles as hellish swindles. But the mass
of believers increased enormously. The revolutionary sect
began to organise. The Sunday sermons of the rebellious
shepherd attracted gatherings of 40,000 and more to Niklashausen.

For several months Hans the Piper preached before the
masses. He did not intend, however, to confine himself to
preaching. He was in secret communication with the priest
of Niklashausen and with two knights, Kunz of Thunfeld
and his son, who accepted the new gospel and were singled

out as the military leaders of the planned insurrection. Finally, on the Sunday preceding the day of St. Kilian, when the shepherd believed his power to be strong enough, he gave the signal. He closed his sermon with the following words: "And now go home, and weigh in your mind what our Holiest Madonna has announced to you, and on the coming Saturday leave your wives and children and old men at home, but you, you men, come back here to Niklashausen on the day of St. Margaret, which is next Saturday, and bring with you your brothers and friends, as many as they may be. Do not come with pilgrims' staves, but covered with weapons and ammunition, in one hand a candle, in the other a sword and a pike or halberd, and the Holy Virgin will then announce to you what she wishes you to do." But before the peasants came in masses, the horsemen of the bishop seized the prophet of rebellion at night, and brought him to the Castle of Wuerzburg. On the appointed day, 34,000 armed peasants appeared, but the news had a discouraging effect on the mass; the majority went home, the more initiated retained about 16,000 with whom they moved to the castle under the leadership of Kunz of Thunfeld and his son Michael. The bishop, by means of promises, persuaded them to go home, but as soon as they began to disperse, they were attacked by the bishop's horsemen, and many were imprisoned. Two were decapitated, and Hans the Piper was burned. Kunz of Thunfeld fled, and was allowed to return only at the price of ceding all his estates to the monastery. Pilgrimages to Niklashausen continued for some time, but were finally suppressed.

After this first attempt, Germany remained quiet for some time; but at the end of the century rebellions and conspiracies of the peasants started anew.

We shall pass over the Dutch peasant revolt of 1491 and 1492 which was suppressed by Duke Albrecht of Saxony in the battle near Heemskerk; also the revolt of the peasants of the Abbey of Kempten in Upper Suabia which occurred simultaneously, and the Frisian revolt under Shaard Ahlva, about 1497, which was also suppressed by Albrecht of Saxony. These revolts were mostly too far from the scene of the actual Peasant War. In part they were struggles of hitherto free peasants against the attempt to force feudalism upon them. We now pass to the two great conspiracies which prepared the Peasant War: the *Union Shoe* and the *Poor Konrad*.

The rise in the price of commodities which had called forth the revolt of the peasants in the Netherlands, brought about, in 1493, in Alsace, a secret union of peasants and plebeians with a sprinkling of the purely middle-class opposition party, and a certain amount of sympathy even among the lower nobility. The seat of the union was the region of Schlettstadt, Sulz, Dambach, Rossheim, Scherweiler, etc. The conspirators demanded the plundering and extermination of the Jews, whose usury then, as now, sucked the blood of the peasants of Alsace, the introduction of a jubilee year to cancel all debts, the abolition of taxes, tolls and other burdens, the abolition of the ecclesiastical and Rottweil (imperial) court, the right to ratify taxation, the reduction of the priests' incomes to a prebend of between fifty and sixty guilders, the abolition of the auricular confession, and the establishment in the communities of courts elected by the communities themselves. The conspirators planned, as soon as they became strong enough, to overpower the stronghold of Schlettstadt, to confiscate the treasuries of the monasteries and the city, and from there to arouse the whole of Alsace. The banner of the union

to be unfurled at the moment of insurrection, contained a
peasant's shoe with long leather strings, the so-called Union
Shoe, which gave a symbol and a name to the peasant conspiracies of the following twenty years.

The conspirators held their meetings at night on the lone-
some Hungerberg. Membership in the Union was connected
with the most mysterious ceremonies and threats of severest
punishment against traitors. Nevertheless, the movement
became known about Easter Week of 1493, the time appointed for the attack on Schlettstadt. The authorities
immediately intervened. Many of the conspirators were
arrested and put on the rack, to be quartered or decapitated. Many were crippled by chopping their hands and
fingers, and driven out of the country. A large number
fled to Switzerland. The Union Shoe, however, was far
from being annihilated and continued its existence in secret.
Numerous exiles, spread over Switzerland and south Germany, became its emissaries. Finding everywhere the same
oppression and the same inclination towards revolt, they
spread the Union Shoe over the territory of present-day
Baden. The greatest admiration is due the tenacity and
endurance with which the peasants of upper Germany con-
spired for thirty years after 1493, with which they over-
came the obstacles to a more centralised organisation in
spite of the fact that they were scattered over the countryside, and with which, after numberless dispersions, defeats, executions of leaders, they renewed their conspiracies
over and over again, until an opportunity came for a mass
upheaval.

In 1502, the bishopric of Speyer, which at that time
embraced also the locality of Bruchsal, showed signs of a
secret movement among the peasants. The Union Shoe had
here reorganised itself with considerable success. About

7,000 men belonged to the organisation whose centre was Untergrombach, between Bruchsal and Weingarten, and whose ramifications reached down the Rhine to the Main, and up to the Margraviate of Baden. Its articles provided: No ground rent, tithe, tax or toll to be paid to the princes, the nobility or the clergy; serfdom to be abolished; monasteries and other church estates to be confiscated and divided among the people, and no other authority to be recognised aside from the emperor.

We find here for the first time expressed among the peasants the two demands of secularising the church estates in favour of the people and of a unified and undivided German monarchy—demands which henceforth will be found regularly in the more advanced faction of the peasants and plebeians.

In Thomas Muenzer's programme, the division of the church estates was tranformed into confiscation in favour of common property, and the unified German *empire*, into the unified and undivided *republic*.

The renewed Union Shoe had, as well as the old, its own secret meeting places, its oath of silence, its initiation ceremonies, and its union banner with the legend, "Nothing but God's Justice." The plan of action was similar to that of the Alsatian Union. Bruchsal, where the majority of the population belonged to the Union, was to be overpowered. A union army was to be organised and dispatched into the surrounding principalities as moving points of concentration.

The plan was betrayed by a clergyman to whom one of the conspirators revealed it in the confessional. The governments immediately resorted to counter action. How widespread the Union had become, is apparent from the terror which seized the various imperial estates in Alsace and in the Union of Suabia. Troops were concentrated, and mass arrests were made. Emperor Maximilian, "the last of the knights," issued the most bloodthirsty, punitive decree against the undertaking of the peasants. Hordes of peasants assembled here and there, and armed resistance was offered, but the isolated peasant troops could not hold ground for a long time. Some of the conspirators were executed and many fled, but the secrecy was so well preserved that the majority, and also the leaders, could remain unmolested in their own localities or in the countries of the neighbouring masters.

After this new defeat, there followed a prolonged period of apparent quiet in the class struggles. The work, however, was continued in an underground way. Already, in the first years of the Sixteenth Century, *Poor Konrad* was formed in Suabia, apparently in connection with the scattered members of the Union Shoe. In the Black Forest, the Union Shoe continued in isolated circles until, ten years later, an energetic peasant leader succeeded in uniting the various threads and combining them into a great conspiracy. Both conspiracies became public, one shortly after the other, in the restless years from 1513 to 1515, in which the Swiss, Hungarian and Slovenian peasants made a series of significant insurrections.

The man who restored the Upper Rhenish Union Shoe was Joss Fritz of Untergrombach, a fugitive from the conspiracy of 1502, a former soldier, in all respects an outstanding figure. After his flight, he had kept himself in various localities between the Lake Constance and the Black Forest, and finally settled as a vassal near Freiburg in Breisgau, where he even became a forester. Interesting details as to the manner in which he reorganised the Union from this point of vantage and as to the skill with which he managed to attract people of different character, are

contained in the investigations. It was due to the diplomatic talent and the untiring endurance of this model con-
spirator that a considerable number of people of the most
divergent classes became involved in the Union: knights,
priests, burghers, plebeians and peasants, and it is almost
certain that he organised several grades of the conspiracy,
one more or less sharply divided from the other.   All
serviceable elements were utilised with the greatest circumspection and skill.   Outside of the initiated emissaries who
wandered over the country in various disguises, the vagrants
and beggars were used for subordinate missions.   Joss stood
in direct communication with the beggar kings, and through
them he held in his hand the numerous vagabond population.   In fact, the beggar kings played a considerable
rôle in his conspiracy.   Very original figures they were,
these beggar kings.   One roamed the country with a girl
using her seemingly wounded feet as a pretext for begging;
he wore more than eight insignia on his hat—the fourteen
deliverers, St. Ottilie, Our Mother in Heaven, etc.; besides,
he wore a long red beard, and carried a big knotty stick
with a dagger and pike.   Another, begging in the name of
St. Velten, offered spices and worm-seeds; he wore a long
iron-coloured coat, a red barret, with the Baby of Trient
attached thereto, a sword at his side, and many knives and
a dagger on his girdle.   Others had artificial open wounds,
besides similar picturesque attire.   There were at least ten
of them, and for the price of two thousand guilders they
were supposed to set fire simultaneously in Alsace, in the
Margraviate of Baden, and in Breisgau, and to put themselves, with at least 2,000 men of their own, under the
command of Georg Schneider, the former Captain of the
Lansquenets, on the day of the Zabern Parish Fair in
Rozen, in order to conquer the city.   A courier service

from station to station was established between real members of the union.   Joss Fritz and his chief emissary, Stoffel
of Freiburg, continually riding from place to place, reviewed
the armies of the neophytes at night.   There is ample
material in the documents of the court investigations relative
to the spread of the Union in the Upper Rhine and Black
Forest regions.   The documents contain many names of
members from the various localities in that region, together with descriptions of persons.   Most of those mentioned were journeymen, peasants and innkeepers, a few
nobles, priests (like that of Lehen himself), and unemployed
Lansquenets.   This composition shows the more developed
character that the Union Shoe had assumed under Joss
Fritz.   The plebeian element of the cities began to assert
itself more and more.   The ramifications of the conspiracy
went over into Alsace, present-day Baden, up to Wuerttemberg and the Main.   Larger meetings were held from time
to time on remote mountains such as the Kniebis, etc., and
the affairs of the Union were discussed.   The meetings of
the chiefs, often participated in by local members as well
as by delegates of the more remote localities, took place
on the Hartmatte near Lehen, and it was here that the
fourteen articles of the Union were adopted: No master
besides the emperor, and (according to some) the pope;
abolition of the Rottweil imperial court; limitation of the
church court to religious affairs; abolition of all interest
which had been paid so long that it equalled the capital;
an interest of 5 per cent as the highest permissible rate;
freedom of hunting, fishing, grazing, and wood cutting;
limitation of the priests to one prebend for each; confiscation of all church estates and monastery gems in favour
of the union; abolition of all inequitable taxes and tolls;
eternal peace within entire Christendom, energetic action

against all opponents of the Union; Union taxes; seizure
of a strong city, such as Freiburg, to serve as the centre
of the Union; opening of negotiations with the emperor as
soon as the Union hordes were gathered, and with Switzerland in case the emperor declined—these were the points
agreed upon. We see that the demands of the peasants
and plebeians assumed a more and more definite and decisive form, although concessions had to be made in the
same measure to the more moderate and timid elements
as well.

The blow was to be struck about Autumn, 1513. Nothing was lacking but a Union banner, and Joss Fritz went
to Heilbrun to have it painted. It contained, besides all
sorts of emblems and pictures, the Union Shoe and the
legend "God help thy divine justice." While he was away,
a premature attempt was made to overwhelm Freiburg, but
the attempt was discovered. Some indiscretions in the
conduct of the propaganda put the council of Freiburg and
the Margrave of Baden on the right track. The betrayal of
two conspirators completed the series of disclosures.
Presently the Margrave, the council of Freiburg, and the
imperial government of Ensisheim sent out their spies and
soldiers. A number of Union members were arrested,
tortured and executed. But the majority escaped once
more, Joss Fritz among them. The Swiss government now
persecuted the fugitives with great assiduity and even executed many of them. However, it could not prevent the
majority of the fugitives from keeping themselves continually in the vicinity of their homes and gradually returning
there. The Alsace government in Ensisheim was more
cruel than the others. It ordered very many to be decapitated, broken on the wheel, and quartered. Joss Fritz kept
himself mainly on the Swiss bank of the Rhine, but he

also went often to the Black Forest without ever being apprehended.

Why the Swiss made common cause with the neighbouring governments this time is apparent from the peasant revolt that broke out the following year, 1514, in Berne, Sollothurne and Lucerne, and resulted in a purging of the aristocratic governments and the institution of patricians. The peasants also forced through some privileges for themselves. If these Swiss local revolts succeeded, it was simply due to the fact that there was still less centralisation in Switzerland than in Germany. The local German masters were all subdued by the peasants of 1525, and if they succumbed, it was due to the organised mass armies of the princes. These latter, however, did not exist in Switzerland.

Simultaneously with the Union Shoe in Baden, and apparently in direct connection with it, a second conspiracy was formed in Wuerttemberg. According to documents, it had existed since 1503, but since the name Union Shoe became too dangerous after the dispersal of the Untergrombach conspirators, it adopted the name of Poor Konrad. Its seat was the valley of Rems underneath the mountain of Hohenstaufen. Its existence had been no mystery for a long time, at least among the people. The shameless pressure of Duke Ulrich's government, and the series of famine years which so greatly aided the outbreaks of 1513 and 1514, had increased the number of conspirators. The newly imposed taxes on wine, meat and bread, as well as a capital tax of one penny yearly for every guilder, caused the new outbreak. The city of Schorndorf, where the heads of the complot used to meet in the house of a cutler named Kaspar Pregizer, was to be seized first. In the spring of 1514, the rebellion broke out. Three thousand, and, according to others, five thousand peasants appeared before

the city, and were persuaded by the friendly promises of
the Duke's officers to move on. Duke Ulrich, having promised the abolition of the new tax, came riding fast with
eighty horsemen, to find that everything was quiet in consequence of the promise. He promised to convene a diet
where all complaints would be examined. The chiefs of the
organisation, however, knew very well that Ulrich sought
only to keep the people quiet until he had recruited and
concentrated enough troops to be able to break his word
and collect the taxes by force. They issued from Kaspar
Pregizer's house, "the office of Poor Konrad," a call to
a Union congress, this call having the support of emissaries
everywhere. The success of the first uprising in the valley
of Rems had everywhere strengthened the movement among
the people. The papers and the emissaries found a favourable response, and so the congress held in Untertuerkhein on
May 28, was attended by numerous representatives from
all parts of Wuerttemberg. It was decided immediately to
proceed with the propaganda and to strike a decisive blow
in the valley of Rems at the first opportunity in order to
spread the uprising from that point in every direction.
While Bantelshans of Dettingen, a former soldier, and
Singerhans of Wuertingen, a prominent peasant, were bring-
ing the Suabian Alp into the Union, the uprising broke out
on every side. Though Singerhans was suddenly attacked
and seized, the cities of Backnang, Winnenden, and Mark-
groenningen fell into the hands of the peasants combined
with the plebeians, and the entire territory from Weinsberg
to Blaubeuren and from there up to the frontiers of Baden,
was in open revolt. Ulrich was compelled to yield. However, while he was calling the Diet for June 25, he sent
out a circular letter to the surrounding princes and free
cities, asking for aid against the uprising, which, he said,

threatened all princes, authorities and nobles in the empire, and which "strangely resembled the Union Shoe."

In the meantime, the Diet, representing the cities, and many delegates of the peasants who also demanded seats in the Diet, convened on June 18 in Stuttgart.

The prelates were not there as yet. The knights had not been invited. The opposition of the city of Stuttgart, as well as two threatening hordes of peasants at Leonberg nearby in the valley of Rems, strengthened the demands of the peasants. Their delegates were admitted, and it was decided to depose and punish three of the hated councillors of the Duke—Lamparter, Thumb and Lorcher, to add to the Duke a council of four knights, four burghers and four peasants, to grant him a civil list, and to confiscate the monasteries and the endowments in favour of the State treasury.

Duke Ulrich met these revolutionary decisions with a coup d'état. On June 21, he rode with his knights and councillors to Tuebingen, where he was followed by the prelates. He ordered the middle-class to come there as well. This was obeyed, and there he continued the session of the Diet without the peasants. The burghers, confronted with military terrorism, betrayed their allies, the peasants. On July 8, the Tuebingen agreement came into being, which imposed on the country almost a million of the Duke's debt, imposed on the Duke some limitations of power which he never fulfilled, and disposed of the peasants with a few meagre general phrases and a very definite penal law against insurrection. Of course, nothing was mentioned about peasant representation in the Diet. The plain people cried "Treason!" but the Duke, having acquired new credits after his debts were taken over by the estates, soon gathered troops while his neighbours, particularly the Elector

Palatine, were sending military aid. Thus, by the end of July, the Tuebingen agreement had been accepted all over the country, and a new oath taken. Only in the valley of Rems did Poor Konrad offer resistance. The Duke, who rode there in person, was almost killed. A peasant camp was formed on the mountain of Koppel. But the affair dragged on, most of the insurgents running away for lack of food; later the remaining ones also went home after concluding an ambiguous agreement with some representatives of the Diet. Ulrich, whose army had in the meantime been strengthened by voluntarily offered troops of the cities which, having attained their demands, now fanatically turned against the peasants, attacked the valley of Rems contrary to the terms of the agreement, and plundered its cities and villages. Sixteen hundred peasants were captured, sixteen of them decapitated, and the rest receiving heavy fines in favour of Ulrich's treasury. Many remained in prison for a long time. A number of penal laws were issued against a renewal of the organisation, against all gatherings of peasants, and the nobility of Suabia formed a special union for the suppression of all attempts at insurrection. Meantime, the chief leaders of Poor Konrad had succeeded in escaping into Switzerland, whence most of them returned home singly, after the lapse of a few years.

Simultaneously with the Wuerttemberg movement, symptoms of new Union Shoe activities became manifest in Breisgau and in the Margraviate of Baden. In June, an insurrection was attempted at Buehl, but it was immediately dispersed by Margrave Philipp—the leader, Gugel-Bastian of Freiburg, having been seized and executed on the block.

In the spring of the same year, 1514, a general peasant war broke out in Hungary. A crusade against the Turks was being preached, and, as usual, freedom was promised to the serfs and bondsmen who would join it. About 60,000 congregated, and were to be under the command of György Dózsa,[16] a Szekler, who had distinguished himself in the preceding Turkish wars and even attained nobility. The Hungarian knights and magnates, however, looked with disfavour upon the crusade which threatened to deprive them of their property and slaves. They hastily followed the individual hordes of peasants, and took back their serfs by force and mistreated them. When the army of crusaders learned about it, all the fury of the oppressed peasants was unleashed. Two of the men, enthusiastic advocates of the crusade, Lawrence Mészáros and Barnabas, fanned the fire, inciting the hatred of the army against the nobility by their revolutionary speeches. Dózsa himself shared the anger of his troops against the treacherous nobility. The army of crusaders became an army of the revolution, and Dózsa assumed leadership of the movement.

He camped with his peasants in the Rakos field near Pest. Hostilities were opened with encounters between the peasants and the people of the nobility in the surrounding villages and in the suburbs of Pest. Soon there were skirmishes, and then followed Sicilian Vespers for all the nobility who fell into the hands of the peasants, and burning of all the castles in the vicinity. The court threatened in vain. When the first acts of the people's justice towards the nobility had been accomplished under the walls of the city, Dózsa proceeded to further operations. He divided his army into five columns. Two were sent to the mountains of Upper Hungary in order to effect an insurrection and to exterminate the nobility. The third, under Ambros Szaleves, a citizen of Pest, remained on the Rakos to guard the capital. The fourth and fifth were led by Dózsa and his brother Gregor against Szegedin.

In the meantime, the nobility gathered in Pest, and called to its aid Johann Zapolya, the *voivode* of Transylvania. The nobility, joined by the middle-class of Budapest, attacked and annihilated the army on the Rakos, after Szaleves with the middle-class elements of the peasant army had gone over to the enemy. A host of prisoners were executed in the most cruel fashion. The rest were sent home minus their noses and ears.

Dózsa suffered defeat before Szegedin and moved to Czanad which he captured, having defeated an army of the nobility under Batory Istvan and Bishop Esakye, and having perpetrated bloody repressions on the prisoners, among them the Bishop and the royal Chancellor Teleky, for the atrocities committed on the Rakos. In Czanad he proclaimed a republic, abolition of the nobility, general equality and sovereignty of the people, and then moved toward Temesvar, to which place Batory had rushed with his army. But during the siege of this fortress which lasted for two months and while he was being reinforced by a new army under Anton Hosza, his two army columns in Upper Hungary suffered defeat in several battles at the hand of the nobility, and Johann Zapolya, with his Transylvanian army, moved against him. The peasants were attacked by Zapolya and dispersed. Dózsa was captured, roasted on a red hot throne, and his flesh eaten by his own people, whose lives were granted to them only under this condition. The dispersed peasants, reassembled by Lawrence and Hosza, were defeated again, and whoever fell into the hands of the enemies were either impaled or hanged. The peasants' corpses hung in thousands along the roads or at the entrances of burned-down villages. According to reports, about 60,000 either fell in battle, or were massacred. The nobility took care that at the next session of the Diet, the enslavement of the peasants should again be recognised as the law of the land.

The peasant revolt in Carinthia, Carniola and Styria, the "windy marshes," which broke out at the same time, originated in a conspiracy akin to the Union Shoe, organised as early as 1503 in that region, wrung dry by imperial officers, devastated by Turkish invasions, and tortured by famines. It was this conspiracy that made the insurrection possible. Already in 1513, the Slovenian as well as the German peasants of this region had once more raised the war banner of the Stara Prawa (The Old Rights). They allowed themselves to be placated that time, and when in 1514 they gathered anew in large masses, they were again persuaded to go home by a direct promise of the Emperor Maximilian to restore the old rights. Still, the war of vengeance by the deceived people broke out in the Spring of 1515 with much more vigour. Here, as in Hungary, castles and monasteries were destroyed, captured nobles being tried and executed by peasant juries. In Styria and Carinthia, the emperor's captain Dietrichstein soon succeeded in crushing the revolt. In Carniola, it could be suppressed only through an attack from the Rain (Autumn, 1516) and through subsequent Austrian atrocities which formed a worthy counterpart to the infamies of the Hungarian nobility.

It is clear why, after a series of such decisive defeats, and after these mass atrocities of the nobility, the German peasants remained quiescent for a long time. Still, neither conspiracies nor local uprisings were totally absent. Already in 1516 most of the fugitives of the Union Shoe and Poor Konrad had returned to Suabia and to the upper

Rhine. In 1517 the Union Shoe was again in full swing in the Black Forest. Joss Fritz himself, who still carried in his bosom the old Union Shoe banner of 1513, traversed the Black Forest in various directions, and developed great activity. The conspiracy was being organised anew. Meetings were again held on the Kniebis as they had been four years before. Secrecy, however, was not maintained. The governments learned the facts and interfered. Many were captured and executed. The most active and intelligent members were compelled to flee, among them Joss Fritz, who, although still not captured, seems, however, to have died in Switzerland a short time afterwards. At any rate, his name is not mentioned again.

FOOT AND MOUNTED
REVOLUTIONARY PEASANTS

CHAPTER IV

WHILE the fourth Union Shoe organisation was being suppressed in the Black Forest, Luther, in Wittenberg, gave the signal to a movement which was destined to draw all the estates into its torrent, and to shake the whole empire. The theses of this Augustinian from Thuringia had the effect of lightning in a powder magazine. The manifold and contradictory strivings of the knights and the middle-class, the peasants and the plebeians, the princes craving for sovereignty, the lower clergy, secretly playing at mysticism and the learned writer's opposition of a satirical and burlesque nature, found in Luther's theses a common expression around which they grouped themselves with astounding rapidity. This alliance of all the opposing elements, though formed overnight and of brief duration, suddenly revealed the enormous power of the movement, and gave it further impetus.

But this very rapid growth of the movement was also destined to develop the seeds of discord which were hidden in it. It was destined to tear asunder at least those portions of the aroused mass which, by their very situation in life, were directly opposed to each other, and to put them in their normal state of mutual hostility. Already in the first years of the Reformation, the assembling of the heterogeneous mass of the opposition around two central points became a fact. Nobility and middle-class grouped themselves unconditionally around Luther. Peasants and plebeians, as yet failing to see in Luther a direct enemy, formed a separate revolutionary party of the opposition. This was nothing new, since now the movement had become much more general, much broader in scope and deeper than it was in the pre-Luther times, which necessarily brought about a sharp antagonism and an open struggle between the two parties. This direct opposition soon became apparent. Luther and Muenzer, fighting in the press and in the pulpit, were as much opposed to each other as were the armies of princes, knights and cities (consisting, as they did, mainly of Lutherans or of forces at least inclined towards Lutherism), and the hordes of peasants and plebeians routed by those armies.

The divergence of interests of the various elements accepting the Reformation became apparent even before the Peasant War in the attempt of the nobility to realise its demands as against the princes and the clergy.

The situation of the German nobility at the beginning of the Sixteenth Century has been depicted above. The nobility was losing its independence to the ever-increasing power of the lay and clerical princes. It realised that in the same degree as it was going down as a group in society, the power of the empire was going down as well, dissolving itself into a number of sovereign principalities. The collapse of the nobility coincided, in its own opinion, with the collapse of the German nation. Added to it was the fact that the nobility, especially that section of it which was under the empire, by virtue of its military occupation and its attitude towards the princes, directly represented the empire and the imperial power. The nobility was the most national of the estates, and it knew that the stronger were the imperial power and the unity of Germany, and the weaker and less numerous the princes, the more powerful would the nobility become. It was for that reason that the knighthood was generally dissatisfied with the pitiful political situation of Germany, with the powerlessness of the empire in foreign affairs, which increased in the same degree as, by inheritance, the court was adding to the empire one province after the other, with the intrigues of foreign powers inside of Germany and with the plottings of German princes with foreign countries against the power of the empire. It was for that reason, also, that the demands of the nobility instantly assumed the form of a demand for the reform of the empire, the victims of which were to be the princes and the higher clergy. Ulrich of Hutten, the theoretician of the German nobility, undertook to formulate this demand in combination with Franz von Sickingen, its military and diplomatic representative.

The reform of the empire as demanded by the nobility was conceived by Hutten in a very radical spirit and expressed very clearly. Hutten demanded nothing else than the elimination of all princes, the secularisation of all church principalities and estates, and the restoration of *a democracy of the nobility* headed by a monarchy,—a form of government reminiscent of the heyday of the late Polish republic. Hutten and Sickingen believed that the empire would again become united, free and powerful, should the rule of the nobility, a predominantly military class, be reestablished, the princes, the elements of disintegration, removed, the power of the priests annihilated, and Germany torn away from under the dominance of the Roman Church.

Founded on serfdom this democracy of the nobility, the prototype of which could be found in Poland and, in the empires conquered by the Germanic tribes, at least in their first centuries, is one of the most primitive forms of society, and its normal course of development is to become an extensive feudal hierarchy, which was a considerable ad-

vance. Such a powerful democracy of the nobility had
already become an impossibility in Germany of the Sixteenth Century, first of all because there existed at that
time important and powerful German cities and there was
no prospect of an alliance between nobility and the cities
such as brought about in England the transformation of
the feudal order into a bourgeois constitutional monarchy.
In Germany, the old nobility survived, while in England
it was exterminated by the Wars of the Roses,[17] only twenty-
eight families remaining, and was superseded by a new
nobility of middle-class derivation and middle-class tendencies. In Germany, serfdom was still the common practice, the nobility drawing its income from *feudal* sources,
while in England serfdom had been virtually eliminated,
and the nobility had become plain middle-class land owners,
with a *middle-class* source of income—the ground rent.
Finally, that centralisation of absolute monarchial power
which in France had existed and kept growing since Louis
XI due to the clash of interests between nobility and
middle-class, was impossible in Germany where conditions
for national centralisation existed in a very rudimentary
form, if at all.

Under these conditions, the greater was Hutten's determination to carry out his ideals in practice, the more concessions was he compelled to make, and the more clouded
did his plan of reforming the empire become. Nobility,
alone, lacked power to put the reform through. This was
manifest from its weakness in comparison with the princes.
Allies were to be looked for, and these could only be found
either in the cities, or among the peasantry and the influential advocates of reform. But the cities knew the nobility
too well to trust them, and they rejected all forms of
alliance. The peasants justly saw in the nobility, which

exploited and mistreated them, their bitterest enemy, and as to the theoreticians of reform, they made common cause with the middle-class, the princes, or the peasants. What advantages, indeed, could the nobility promise the middle-class or the peasants from a reform of the empire whose main task it was to lift the nobility into a higher position? Under these circumstances Hutten could only be silent in his propaganda writings about the future interrelations between the nobility, the cities and the peasants, or to mention them only briefly, putting all evils at the feet of the princes, the priests, and the dependence upon Rome, and showing the middle-class that it was in their interests to remain at least neutral in the coming struggle between the nobility and the princes. No mention was ever made by Hutten of abolishing serfdom or other burdens imposed upon the peasants by the nobility.

The attitude of the German nobility towards the peasants of that time was exactly the same as that of the Polish nobility towards its peasants in the insurrections since 1830. As in the modern Polish upheavals, the movement could have been brought to a successful conclusion only by an alliance of all the opposition parties, mainly the nobility and the peasants. But of all alliances, this one was entirely impossible on either side. The nobility was not ready to give up its political privileges and its feudal rights over the peasants, while the revolutionary peasants could not be drawn by vague prospects into an alliance with the nobility, the class which was most active in their oppression. The nobility could not win over the German peasant in 1522, as it failed in Poland in 1830. Only total abolition of serfdom, bondage and all privileges of nobility could have united the rural population with it. The nobility, like every privileged class, had not, however, the slightest desire to

give up its privileges, its favourable situation, and the
major parts of its sources of income.

Thus it came about that when the struggle broke out,
the nobles were alone in the field against the princes. It
was obvious that the princes, who, for two centuries had
been taking the ground from under the nobility's feet, would
this time also gain a victory without much effort.

The course of the struggle itself is well known. Hutten
and Sickingen, already recognised as the political and military chiefs of the middle German nobility, organised in
Landau, in 1522, a union of the Rhenish, Suabian and
Franconian nobility for the duration of six years, ostensibly
for self-defense. Sickingen assembled an army, partly out
of his own means and partly in combination with the neighbouring knights. He organised the recruiting of armies and
reinforcements in Franconia, along the Lower Rhine, in the
Netherlands and in Westphalia, and in September, 1522, he
opened hostilities by declaring a feud against the Elector-
Archbishop of Trier. While he was stationed near Trier,
his reinforcements were cut off by a quick intervention of
the princes. The Landgrave of Hesse and the Elector
Palatine went to the aid of the Archbishop of Trier, and
Sickingen was hastily compelled to retreat to his castle,
Landstuhl. In spite of all the efforts of Hutten and the
remainder of his friends, the united nobility, intimidated by
the concentrated and quick action of the princes, left him
in the lurch. Sickingen was mortally wounded, surrendered
Landstuhl, and soon afterwards he died. Hutten was compelled to flee to Switzerland, where he died a few months
later on the Isle of Ufnau, on the Lake of Zurich.

With this defeat, and with the death of both leaders,
the power of the nobility as a body, independent of the
princes, was broken. From then on the nobility appeared

only in the service and under the leadership of the princes. The Peasant War, which soon broke out, drove the nobles still more deeply under the direct or indirect protection of the princes. It proved that the German nobility preferred to continue the exploitation of the peasants under princely sovereignty, rather than overthrow the princes and priests through an open alliance with the *emancipated* peasants.

ARMED FRANCONIAN PEASANTS

From a drawing by Albrecht Dürer

CHAPTER V

FROM the moment when Luther's declaration of war against the Catholic hierarchy set into motion all the opposition elements of Germany, not a year passed without the peasants coming forth with their demands. Between 1518 and 1523, one local revolt followed another in the Black Forest and in upper Suabia. Beginning in the Spring of 1524, these revolts assumed a systematic character. In April of that year, the peasants of the Abbey of Marchthal refused serf labour and duties; in May of the same year, the peasants of St. Blasien refused serf payments; in June, the peasants of Steinheim near Memmingen declared they would pay neither the tithe nor other duties; in July and August, the peasants of Thurgau rebelled and were quieted partly through the mediation of Zurich, partly through the brutality of the confederacy which executed many of them. Finally, a decisive uprising took place in the Margraviate of Stuehlingen, which may be looked upon as the *real beginning of the Peasant War*.

The peasants of Stuehlingen suddenly refused deliveries to the Landgrave and assembled in strong numbers. On October 24, 1524, they moved towards Waldshut under Hans Mueller of Bulgenbach. Here they organised an evangelical fraternity, jointly with the city middle-class. The latter joined the organisation the more willingly since they were in conflict with the government of Upper Austria over the religious persecutions of their preacher, Balthaser Hubmaier, a friend and disciple of Thomas Muenzer's. A union tax of three kreutzer weekly was imposed. It was an enormous sum for the value of money of that time. Emissaries were sent out to Alsace, to the Moselle, to the entire Upper Rhine and to Franconia, to bring peasants everywhere into the Union. The aims of the Union were proclaimed as follows: abolition of feudal power; destruction of all castles and monasteries; elimination of all masters outside of the emperor. The German tricolour was the banner of the Union.

The uprising spread rapidly over the entire territory of present-day Baden. A panic seized the nobility of Upper Suabia, whose military forces were all engaged in Italy, in a war against Francis I of France. Nothing remained for it but to gain time by protracted negotiations, meanwhile collecting money and recruiting troops, pending the moment when it would feel strong enough to punish the peasants for their audacity by "burning and scorching, plundering and murdering." From that moment there began that systematic betrayal, that consistent recourse to perfidiousness and secret malice, which distinguished the nobility and the princes throughout the entire Peasant War, and which was their strongest weapon against decentralised peasants. The Suabian Union, comprising the princes, the nobility, and the imperial cities of Southwest Germany, tried conciliatory measures without guaranteeing the peasants real concessions. The latter continued their movement. Hans Mueller of Bulgenbach marched, from September 30 to the middle of October, through the Black Forest up to Urach and Furtwangen, increased his troops to 3,500 and took a position near Eratingen, not far from Stuehlingen. The nobility had no more than 1,700 men at their disposal, and even those were divided. It had to agree to an armistice, which was concluded in the camp at Eratingen. The peasants were promised a peaceful agreement, either directly between the interested parties, or by means of an arbitrator, and an investigation of complaints by the court at Stockach. The troops of both the nobility and the peasants were dispersed.

The peasants formulated sixteen articles, the acceptance of which was to be demanded of the court at Stockach. The articles were very moderate. They included abolition of the hunting right, of serf labour, of excessive taxes and master privileges in general, protection against wilful arrests and against partisan courts. The peasants' demands went no farther.

Nevertheless, immediately after the peasants went home, the nobility demanded continuation of all contested services pending the court decision. The peasants refused, advising the masters to go to the court. Thus the conflict was renewed, the peasants reassembled, and the princes and masters once again concentrated their troops. This time the movement spread far over the Breisgau and deep into Wuerttemberg. The troops under Georg Truchsess of Waldburg, the Alba of the Peasant War, observed the peasants' movements, attacked individual reinforcements, but did not dare to attack the main force. Georg Truchsess negotiated with the peasant chiefs, and here and there he effected agreements.

By the end of December, proceedings began before the court at Stockach. The peasants protested against the court, composed entirely of nobles. In reply, an imperial edict to this effect was read. The proceedings lagged, while the nobility, the princes and the Suabian Union authorities were arming themselves. Archduke Ferdinand who dominated, besides hereditary lands then still belonging to Austria, also Wuerttemberg, the Black Forest and Southern

Alsace, ordered the greatest severity against the rebellious peasants. They were to be captured, mercilessly tortured and killed; they were to be exterminated in the most expeditious manner; their possessions to be burned and devastated, and their wives and children driven from the land. It was in that way that the princes and masters kept the armistice, and this is what passed for amicable arbitration and investigation of grievances. Archduke Ferdinand, to whom the house of Welser of Augsburg advanced money, armed himself very carefully. The Suabian Union ordered a special tax, and a contingent of troops to be called in three installments.

The foregoing rebellions coincided with the five months' presence of Thomas Muenzer in the Highland. Though there are no direct proofs of his influence over the outbreak and the course of the movement, it is, nevertheless, indirectly ascertained. The most outspoken revolutionaries among the peasants were mostly his disciples, defending his ideas. The Twelve Articles, as well as the Letter of Articles of the Highland peasants, were ascribed to him by all the contemporaries, although the first was certainly not composed by Muenzer. Already, on his way back to Thuringia, he issued a decisive revolutionary manifesto to the insurgent peasants.

Duke Ulrich, who, since 1519, had been an exile from Wuerttemberg, was now intriguing to regain his land with the aid of the peasants. Since the beginning of his exile he had been trying to utilise the revolutionary party, and had supported it continuously. In most of the local disturbances taking place between 1520 and 1524 in the Black Forest and in Wuerttemberg, his name appeared. Now he armed himself directly for an attack on Wuerttemberg to be launched out of his castle, Hohentweil. However, he was only utilised by the peasants without influencing them, and without enjoying their confidence.

The winter passed without anything decisive happening on either side. The princely masters were in hiding. The peasant revolt was gaining scope. In January, 1525, the entire country between the Danube, the Rhine and the Lech, was in a state of fermentation. In February, the storm broke. While the Black Forest Hegau troops, under Hans Mueller of Bulgenbach, were conspiring with Ulrich of Wuerttemberg, partly sharing his futile march on Stuttgart (February and March, 1525), the peasants arose on February 9 in Ried above Ulm, assembled in a camp near Baltringen which was protected by marshes, hoisted the red flag, and formed, under the leadership of Ulrich Schmid, the Baltringen troop. They were 10,000 to 12,000 strong.

On February 25, the Upper Allgaeu troops, 7,000 strong, assembled at Schusser, moved by the rumour that troops were marching against the dissatisfied elements who had appeared in this locality as everywhere else. The people of Kempten, who had conducted a fight against their archbishop throughout the winter, assembled on the 26th and joined the peasants. The cities of Memmingen and Kaufbeuren joined the movement on certain conditions. The ambiguity of the position of the cities in this movement was already apparent. On March 7, the twelve Memmingen articles were proclaimed in Memmingen for all the peasants of Upper Allgaeu.

A message from the Allgaeu peasants brought about the formation on Lake Constance of the Lake Troop under Eitel Hans. This troop also grew fast. Its headquarters were in Bermatingen.

The peasants also arose in Lower Allgaeu in the region of Ochsenhausen and Schellenberg, in the localities of Zeil and Waldburg, and in the estates of Truchsess. The movement started in the early days of March. This Lower Allgaeu troop, which consisted of 7,000 men, camped near Wurzach.

All these troops adopted the Memmingen articles, which, it must be noted, were still more moderate than the Hegau articles, manifesting, as they did, a remarkable lack of determination in points relating to the attitude of the armed troops towards the nobility and the governments. Such determination, wherever manifested, appeared only in the later stages of the war, when the peasants learned to know from experience the mode of action of their enemies.

A sixth troop was formed on the Danube, simultaneously with the others. From the entire region, Ulm to Donauwoerth, from the valleys of the Iller, Roth and Biber, the peasants came to Leipheim, and opened camp there. From fifteen localities, every able-bodied man had come, while reinforcements were drawn from 117 places. The leader of the Leipheim troop was Ulrich Schoen. Its preacher was Jakob Wehe, the priest of Leipheim.

Thus, at the beginning of March, there were between 30,000 and 40,000 insurgent peasants of Upper Suabia in six camps under arms. The peasant troops were a heterogeneous lot. Muenzer's revolutionary party was everywhere in the minority but it formed the backbone of the peasant camps. The mass of the peasants were always ready to venture compacts with the masters wherever they were promised those concessions which they hoped to force upon their enemies by their menacing attitude. Moreover, as the uprising dragged on and the princes' armies began to approach, the peasants became weary. Most of those who still had something to lose, went home. Added to all the difficulties was the fact that the vagabond masses of the low grade proletariat had joined the troops. This made discipline more difficult, and demoralised the peasants, as the vagabonds were an unreliable element, coming and going all the time. This, alone, is sufficient explanation why, at the beginning, the peasants remained everywhere on the defensive, why they were becoming demoralised in their camps, and why, aside from tactical shortcomings and the rarity of good leaders, they could not match the armies of the princes.

While the troops were assembling, Duke Ulrich invaded Wuerttemberg from Hohentweil with recruited troops and a number of Hegau peasants. Were the peasants now to proceed from the other side, from Waldburg against Truchsess' troops, the Suabian Union would have been lost. But because of the defensive attitude of the peasant troops, Truchsess soon succeeded in concluding an armistice with those of Baltringen, Allgaeu, and the Lake, starting negotiations and fixing a date for terminating the whole undertaking, namely, Judica Sunday (April 2). In the meantime, he was able to proceed against Duke Ulrich, to besiege Stuttgart, compelling him to leave Wuerttemberg as early as March 17. Then he turned against the peasants, but the Lansquenets revolted in his own army and refused to proceed against the peasants. Truchsess succeeded in placating the disgruntled soldiers and moved towards Ulm, where new reinforcements were being gathered. He left an observation post at Kirchheim under the supervision of Teck.

At last the Suabian Union, with free hands and in command of the first contingents, threw off its mask, declaring itself "to be ready, with arms in hand and with the aid of God, to change that which the peasants wilfully ventured."

The peasants adhered strictly to the armistice. On Judica Sunday they submitted their demands, the famous Twelve Articles, for consideration. They demanded the election and removal of clergymen by the communities; the abolition of the small tithe and the utilisation of the large tithe, after subtraction of the priests' salaries, for public purposes; the abolition of serfdom, of fishing and hunting rights, and of death tolls; the limitation of excessive bonded labour, taxes and ground rents; the restitution of the forests, meadows and privileges forcibly withdrawn from the communities and individuals, and the elimination of wilfulness in the courts and the administration. It is obvious that the moderate conciliatory section still had the upper hand among the peasant troops. The revolutionary party had formulated its programme earlier, in the *Letter of Articles*. It was an open letter to all the peasantry, admonishing them to join "the Christian Alliance and Brotherhood" for the purpose of removing all burdens either by goodness, "which will hardly happen," or by force, and threatening all those who refuse to join with the "lay anathema," that is, with expulsion from the society and from any intercourse with the Union members. All castles, monasteries and priests' endowments were also, according to the Letter, to be placed under lay anathema unless the nobility, the priests and the monks relinquished them of their own accord, moved into ordinary houses like other people, and joined the Christian Alliance. We see that this radical manifesto which obviously had been composed *before* the Spring insurrection of 1525, deals in the first place with the revolution, with complete victory over the ruling classes, and that the "lay anathema" only designates those oppressors and traitors that were to be killed, the castles that were to be burned, and the monasteries and endow-

ments that were to be confiscated, their jewels to be turned
into cash.

Before the peasants succeeded in presenting their Twelve
Articles to the proper courts of arbitration, they learned
that the agreement had been broken by the Suabian Union
and that its troops were approaching. Steps were taken
immediately by the peasants. A general meeting of all
Allgaeu, Baltringen and Lake peasants was held at Geis-
beuren. The four divisions were combined and reorganised
into four columns. A decision was made to confiscate the
church estates, to sell their jewels in favour of the war
chest, and to burn the castles. Thus, aside from the official
Twelve Articles, the Letter of the Articles became the rule
of warfare, and Judica Sunday, designated for the conclusion of peace negotiations, became *the date of general
uprising*.

The growing agitation everywhere, the continued local
conflicts of the peasants with the nobility, the news of a
growing revolt in the Black Forest for the preceding six
months and of its spread up to the Danube and the Lech,
are sufficient to explain the rapid succession of peasant
revolts in two-thirds of Germany. The fact, however, that
the partial revolts took place simultaneously, proves that
there were men at the head of the movement who had
organised it through Anabaptists and other emissaries.
Already in the second half of March, disorders broke out
in Wuerttemberg, in the lower regions of the Neckar and
the Odenwald, and in Upper and Middle Franconia. April
2, Judica Sunday, however, had already been named everywhere as the day of the general uprising, and everywhere
the decisive blow, the revolt of the masses, fell in the first
week of April. The Allgaeu, Hegau and Lake peasants
sounded the alarm bells on April 1, calling into the camp

a mass meeting of all able-bodied men, and together with the Baltringen peasants, they immediately opened hostilities against the castles and monasteries.

In Franconia, where the movement was grouped around six centres, the insurrection broke out everywhere in the first days of April. In Noerdlingen two peasant camps were formed about that time, and the revolutionary party of the city under Anton Forner, aided by the peasants, gained the upper hand, appointing Forner the Mayor, and completing a union between the city and the peasants. In the region of Anspach, the peasants revolted everywhere between April 1 and 7, and from here the revolts spread as far as Bavaria. In the region of Rottenburg, the peasants were already under arms on March 22. In the city of Rottenburg the rule of the honourables was overthrown by the lower middle-class and plebeians under Stephan of Menzingen, but since the peasant dues were the chief source of revenue for the city, the new government was able to maintain a vacillating and equivocal attitude towards the peasants. In the Grand Chapter of Wurzburg there was a general uprising, early in April, of the peasants and the small cities. In the bishopric of Bamberg, a general insurrection compelled the bishop to yield within five days. In the North, on the border of Thuringia, the strong Bildhausen Peasant Camp was organised.

In the Odenwald, where Wendel Hipler, a noble and former chancellor of the Count of Hohenlohe, and Georg Metzler, an innkeeper at Ballenberg near Krautheim, were at the head of the revolutionary party, the storm broke out on March 26. The peasants marched from all directions towards the Tauber. Two thousand men from the Rottenburg camp joined. Georg Metzler took command, and having received all reinforcements, marched on April

4 to the monastery of Schoenthal on the Jaxt, where he was joined by the peasants of the Neckar valley. The latter, led by Jaecklein Rohrbach, an innkeeper at Boeckingen near Heilbronn, had proclaimed, on Judica Sunday, the insurrection in Flein, Southeim, etc., while, simultaneously, Wendel Hipler, with a number of conspirators, took Oehringen by surprise and drew the surrounding peasants into the movement. In Schoenthal, the two peasant columns, combined into the Gay Troop, accepted the Twelve Articles, and organised expeditions against the castles and monasteries. The Gay Troop was about 8,000 strong, and possessed cannon, as well as 3,000 guns. Florian Geyer, a Franconian knight, also joined the troop and formed the Black Host, a select division which had been recruited mainly from the Rottenburg and Oehringen infantry.

The Wuerttemberg magistrate in Neckarsulm, Count Ludwig von Helfenstein, opened hostilities. Without much ado, he ordered all peasants that fell into his hands to be executed. The Gay Troop marched against him. The peasants were embittered by the massacres as well as by news of the defeat of the Leipheim Troop, of Jakob Wehe's execution, and the Truchsess atrocities. Von Helfenstein, who had precipitously moved into Weinsberg, was there attacked. The castle was stormed by Florian Geyer. The city was won after a prolonged struggle, and Count Ludwig was taken prisoner, as were several knights. On the following day, April 17, Jaecklein Rohrbach, together with the most resolute members of the troop, held court over the prisoners, and ordered fourteen of them, with von Helfenstein at the head, to run the gauntlet, this being the most humiliating death he could invent for them. The capture of Weinsberg and the terroristic revenge of Jaecklein against von Helfenstein, did not fail to influence the nobility. Count von Loebenstein joined the Peasant Alliance. The Counts von Hohenlohe, who had joined previously without offering any aid, immediately sent the desired cannon and powder.

The chiefs debated among themselves whether they should not make Goetz von Berlichingen their commander "since he could bring to them the nobility." The proposal found sympathy, but Florian Geyer, who saw in this mood of the peasants and their chiefs the beginning of reaction, seceded from the troop, and together with his Black Host, marched first through the Neckar Region, then the Wuerzburg territory, everywhere destroying castles and priests' nests.

The remainder of the troop marched first towards Heilbronn. In this powerful and free imperial city, the patriciate was confronted, as almost everywhere, by a middle-class and revolutionary opposition. The latter, in secret agreement with the peasants, opened the gates before G. Metzler and Jaecklein Rohrbach, on April 17, in the course of a general disturbance. The peasant chiefs with their people took possession of the city. They accepted membership in the brotherhood, and delivered 12,000 guilders in money and a squad of volunteers. Only the possessions of the clergy and the Teutonic Order were pillaged. On the 22d, the peasants moved away, leaving a small garrison. Heilbronn was designated as the centre of the various troops, the latter actually sending delegates and conferring over common actions and common demands of the peasantry. But the middle-class opposition and the honourables who had joined them after the peasant invasion, regained the upper hand in the city, preventing it from taking decisive steps and only waiting for the approach of the princes' troops in order to betray the peasants definitely.

The peasants marched toward the Odenwald. Goetz von Berlichingen who, a few days previous, had offered himself to the Grand Elector Palatine, then to the peasantry, then again to the Grand Elector, was compelled on April 24 to join the Evangelist Fraternity, and to take over the supreme command of the Gay Bright Troop (in contrast to the Black Troop of Florian Geyer). At the same time, however, he was the prisoner of the peasants who mistrusted him and bound him to a council of chiefs without whom he could undertake nothing. Goetz and Metzler moved with a mass of peasants over Buchen to Armorbach, where they remained from April 30, until May 5, arousing the entire region of the Main. The nobility was everywhere compelled to join, and thus its castles were spared. Only the monasteries were burned and pillaged. The troops had obviously become demoralised. The most energetic men were away, either under Florian Geyer or under Jaecklein Rohrbach, who, after the capture of Heilbronn, also separated himself from the troops, apparently because he, judge of Count von Helfenstein, could no longer remain with a body which was in favour of reconciliation with the nobility. This insistence on an understanding with the nobility was in itself a sign of demoralisation. Later, Wendel Hipler proposed a very fitting reorganisation of the troops. He suggested that the Lansquenets, who offered themselves daily, should be drawn into the service, and that the troops should no longer be renewed monthly by assembling fresh contingents and dismissing old ones, but that those of them who had received more or less military training should be retained. The community assembly rejected both proposals. The peasants had become arrogant, viewing the entire war as nothing but a pillage. They wanted to be free to go home as soon as their pockets were full, but the competition of the Lansquenets promised them little. In Amorbach, it went so far that Hans Berlin, a member of the council of Heilbronn, induced the chiefs and the councils of the troops to accept the *Declaration of the Twelve Articles*, a document wherein the remaining sharp edges of the Twelve Articles were removed, and in which, a language of humble supplication was put into the mouths of the peasants. This was too much for the peasants, who rejected the Declaration under great tumult, and insisted on the retention of the original Articles.

In the meantime, a decisive change had taken place in the region of Wuerzburg. The bishop who, after the first uprising early in April, had withdrawn to the fortified Frauenberg near Wuerzburg, from there to send unsuccessful letters in all directions asking for aid, was finally compelled to make temporary concessions. On May 2, a Diet was opened with the peasants represented, but before any results could be achieved, letters were intercepted which proved the bishop's traitorous machinations. The Diet immediately dispersed, and hostilities broke out anew between the insurgent city inhabitants and the peasants on one hand, and the bishop's forces on the other. The bishop fled to Heidelberg on May 5, and on the following day Florian Geyer, with the Black Troop, appeared in Wuerzburg and with him the Franconian Tauber Troop which consisted of the peasants of Mergentheim, Rottenburg and Anspach. On May 7, Goetz von Berlichingen with his Gay Bright Troops came, and the siege of Frauenberg began.

In the vicinity of Limpurg and in the region of Ellwangen and Hall, another contingent was formed by the end of March and the beginning of April, that of Gaildorf or the Common Gay Troop. Its actions were very violent. It aroused the entire region, burned many monasteries and

castles, including the castle of Hohenstaufen, compelled all
the peasants to join it, and compelled all nobles, even the
cup-bearers of Limpurg, to enter the Christian Alliance.
Early in May it invaded Wuerttemberg, but was persuaded
to withdraw. The separatism of the German system of
small states stood then, as in 1848, in the way of a common
action of the revolutionaries of the various state territories. The Gaildorf troop, limited to a small area, was
naturally bound to disperse when all resistance within that
area was broken. The members of this troop concluded
an agreement with the city of Gmuend, and leaving only
500 under arms, they went home.

In the Palatinate, peasant troops were formed on either
bank of the Rhine by the end of April. They destroyed
many castles and monasteries, and on May 1 they took
Neustadt on the Hardt. The Bruchrain peasants, who
appeared in this region, had on the previous day forced
Speyer to conclude an agreement. The Marshal of Zabern,
with the few troops of the Elector, was powerless against
them, and on May 10 the Elector was compelled to conclude an agreement with the peasants, guaranteeing them a
redress of their grievances, to be effected by a Diet.

In Wuerttemberg the revolt had occurred early in separate localities. As early as February, the peasants of the
Urach Alp formed a union against the priests and masters,
and by the end of March the peasants of Blaubeuer, Urach,
Muensingen, Balingen and Rosenfeld revolted. The Wuerttemberg region was invaded by the Gaildorf troop at Goep-
pingen, by Jaecklein Rohrbach at Brackenheim, and by the
remnants of the vanquished Leipheim troop at Pfuelingen.
All these newcomers aroused the rural population. There
were also serious disturbances in other localities. On April
6, Pfuelingen capitulated before the peasants. The gover=

ment of the Austrian Archduke was in a very difficult situation. It had no money and but few troops. The cities and castles were in a bad condition, lacking garrisons or munitions, and even Asperg was practically defenseless. The attempt of the government to call out city reserves against the peasants, decided its temporary defeat. On April 16 the reserves of the city of Bottwar refused to obey orders, marching, instead of to Stuttgart, to Wunnenstein near Bottwar, where they formed the nucleus of a camp of middle-class people and peasants, and added other numbers rapidly. On the same day the rebellion broke out in Zabergau. The monastery of Maulbronn was pillaged, and a number of monasteries and castles were ruined. The Gaeu peasants received reinforcements from the neighbouring Bruchrain.

The command of the Wunnenstein troop was taken by Matern Feuerbacher, a councillor of the city of Bottwar, one of the leaders of the middle-class opposition compromised enough to be compelled to join the peasants. In spite of his new affiliations, however, he remained very moderate, prohibiting the application of the Letter of Articles to the castles, and seeking everywhere to reconcile the peasants with the moderate middle-class. He prevented the amalgamation of the Wuerttemberg peasants with the Gay Bright Troop, and afterwards he also persuaded the Gaildorf troop to withdraw from Wuerttemberg. On April 19 he was deposed in consequence of his middle-class tendencies, but the next day he was again made commander. He was indispensable, and even when Jaecklein Rohrbach came, on April 22, with 200 of his associates to join the Wuerttemberg peasants, he could do nothing but leave Feuerbacher in his place of commander, confining himself to rigid supervision of his actions.

On April 18, the government attempted to negotiate with the peasants stationed at Wunnenstein. The peasants insisted upon acceptance of the Twelve Articles, but this the government's representatives refused to do. The troop now proceeded to act. On April 20, it reached Laufen, where, for the last time, it rejected the offers of the government delegates. On April 22, the troops, numbering 6,000, appeared in Bietighein, threatening Stuttgart. Most of the city council had fled, and a citizens' committee was placed at the head of the administration. The citizenry here was divided, as elsewhere, between the parties of the honourables, the middle-class opposition, and the revolutionary plebeians. On April 25, the latter opened the gates for the peasants, and Stuttgart was immediately garrisoned by them. Here the organisation of the Gay Christian Troop (as the Wuerttemberg insurgents called themselves) was perfected, and rules and regulations were established for remuneration, division of booty and alimentation. A detachment of Stuttgarters, under Theus Gerber, joined the troops.

On April 29, Feuerbacher with all his men marched against the Gaildorf troops, which had entered the Wuerttemberg region at Schorndorf. He drew the entire region into his alliance and thus persuaded the Gaildorf troops to withdraw. In this way, he prevented the revolutionary elements of his men under Rohrbach from combining with the reckless troops of Gaildorf and thus receiving a dangerous reinforcement. Having been informed of Truchsess' approach, he left Schorndorf to meet him, and on May 1 encamped near Kirchheim under Teck.

We have thus traced the origin and the development of the insurrection in that portion of Germany which must be considered the territory of the first group of peasant armies.

Before we proceed to the other groups (Thuringia and Hesse, Alsace, Austria and the Alps) we must give an account of the military operations of Truchsess, in which he, alone at the beginning, later supported by various princes and cities, annihilated the first group of insurgents. We left Truchsess near Ulm, where he came by the end of March, having left an observation corps under Teck, under the command of Dietrich Spaet. Truchsess' corps which together with the Union reinforcements concentrated in Ulm counted hardly 10,000, among them 7,200 infantrymen, was the only army at his disposal capable of an offensive against the peasants. Reinforcements came to Ulm very slowly, due in part to the difficulties of recruiting in insurgent localities, in part to the lack of money in the hands of the government, and also to the fact that the few available troops were everywhere indispensable for garrisoning the fortresses and the castles. We have already observed what a small number of troops were at the disposal of the princes and cities that did not belong to the Suabian Union. Everything depended upon the successes which Georg Truchsess with his union army would score.

Truchsess turned first against the Baltringen troops which, in the meantime, had begun to destroy castles and monasteries in the vicinity of Ried. The peasants who, with the approach of the Union troops withdrew into Ried, were driven out of the marshes by an enveloping movement, crossed the Danube and ran into the ravines and forests of the Suabian Alps. In this region, where cannon and cavalry, the main source of strength of the Union army, were of little avail, Truchsess did not pursue them further. He marched instead against the Leipheim troops which numbered 5,000 men stationed at Leipheim, 4,000 in the valley of Mindel, and 6,000 at Illertissen, and was arousing the en-

tire region, destroying monasteries and castles, and preparing
to march against Ulm with its three columns. It seems
that a certain demoralisation had set in among the peasants
of this division, which had undermined their military morale,
for Jakob Wehe tried at the very beginning to negotiate
with Truchsess. The latter, however, now backed by sufficient military power, declined negotiations, and on April 4
attacked the main troops at Leipheim and entirely disrupted them. Jakob Wehe and Ulrich Schoen, together
with two other peasant leaders, were captured and beheaded. Leipheim capitulated, and after a few marches
through the surrounding country, the entire region was
subdued.

A new rebellion of the Lansquenets, caused by a demand
for plunder and additional remuneration, again stopped
Truchsess' activities until April 10, when he marched southwest against the Baltringen troop which in the meantime
had invaded his estates, Waldburg, Zeil and Wolfegg, and
besieged his castles. Here, also, he found the peasants disunited, and defeated them, on April 11 and 12, one after
the other, in various encounters which completely disrupted
the Baltringen troops. Its remnants withdrew under the
command of the priest Florian, and joined the Lake troops.
Truchsess now turned against the latter. The Lake troops
which in the meantime had made not only military marches
but had also drawn the cities Buchhorn (Friedrichshafen)
and Wollmatingen into the fraternity, held, on April 13, a
big military council in the monastery of Salem, and decided
to move against Truchsess. Alarm bells were sounded and
10,000 men, joined by the defeated remnants of the Baltringen troops, assembled in the camp of Bermatingen. On
April 15 they stood their own in a combat with Truchsess,
who did not wish to risk his army in a decisive battle, pre-

ferring to negotiate, the more so since he received news of the approach of the Allgaeu and Hegau troops. On April 17, in Weingarten, he concluded an agreement with the Lake and Baltringen peasants which seemed quite favourable to them, and which they accepted without suspicion. He also induced the delegates of the Upper and Lower Allgaeu peasants to accept the agreement, and then moved towards Wuerttemberg.

Truchsess' cunning saved him here from certain ruin. Had he not succeeded in fooling the weak, limited, for the most part demoralised peasants and their usually incapable, timid and venal leaders, he would have been closed in with his small army between four columns numbering at least from 25,000 to 30,000 men, and would have perished. It was the narrow-mindedness of his enemies, always inevitable among the peasant masses, that made it possible for him to dispose of them at the very moment when, with one blow, they could have ended the entire war, at least as far as Suabia and Franconia were concerned. The Lake peasants adhered to the agreement, which finally turned out to be their undoing, so rigidly that they later took up arms against their allies, the Hegau peasants. And although the Allgaeu peasants, involved in the betrayal by their leaders, soon renounced the agreement, Truchsess was then out of danger.

The Hegau peasants, though not included in the Weingarten agreement, gave a new example of the appalling narrow-mindedness and the stubborn provincialism which ruined the entire Peasant War. When, after unsuccessful negotiations with them, Truchsess moved towards Wuerttemberg, they followed him, continually pressing his flank, but it did not occur to them to unite with the Wuerttemberg Gay Christian Troop, because previously the peasants of

Wuerttemberg and the Neckar valley refused to come to their assistance. When Truchsess had moved far enough from their home country, they returned peacefully and marched to Freiburg.

We left the Wuerttemberg peasants under the command of Matern Feuerbacher at Kirchheim below Teck, from where the observation corps left by Truchsess had withdrawn towards Urach under the command of Dietrich Spaet. After an unsuccessful attempt to take Urach, Feuerbacher turned towards Nuertingen, sending letters to all neighbouring insurgent troops, calling reinforcements for the decisive battle. Considerable reinforcements actually came from the Wuerttemberg lowlands as well as from Gaeu. The Gaeu peasants had grouped themselves around the remnants of the Leipheim troop which had withdrawn to West Wuerttemberg, and they aroused the entire valleys of Neckar and Nagoldt up to Boeblingen and Leonberg. Those Gaeu peasants, on May 5, came in two strong columns to join Feuerbacher at Nuertingen. Truchsess met the united troops at Boetlingen. Their number, their cannon and their position perplexed him. As usual, he started negotiations and concluded an armistice with the peasants. But as soon as he had thus secured his position, he attacked them on May 12 *during the armistice,* and forced a decisive battle upon them. The peasants offered a long and brave resistance until finally Boetlingen was surrendered to Truchsess owing to the betrayal of the middle-class. The left wing of the peasants, deprived of its base of support, was forced back and encompassed. This decided the battle. The undisciplined peasants were thrown into disorder and, later, into a wild flight, those that were not killed or captured by the horsemen of the Union threw away their weapons and went home. The Bright Christian Troop, and with it the entire Wuerttemberg insurrection was gone.   Theus Gerber fled to Esslingen, Feuerbacher fled to Switzerland, Jaecklein Rohrbach was captured and dragged in chains to Neckargartach, where Truchsess ordered him chained to a post, surrounded by firewood and roasted to death on a slow fire, while he, feasting with horsemen, gloated over this noble spectacle.

From Neckargartach, Truchsess gave aid to the operations of the Elector Palatine by invading Kraichgau. Having received word of Truchsess' successes, the Elector, who meanwhile had gathered troops, immediately broke his agreement with the peasants, attacked Bruchrain on May 23, captured and burned Malsch after vigorous resistance, pillaged a number of villages, and garrisoned Bruchsal. At the same time Truchsess attacked Eppingen and captured the chief of the local movement, Anton Eisenhut, whom the Elector immediately executed with a dozen other peasant leaders.   Bruchrain and Kraichgau were thus subjugated and compelled to pay an indemnity of about 40,000 guilders. Both armies, that of Truchsess now reduced to 6,000 men in consequence of the preceding battles, and that of the Elector (6,500 men), united and moved towards the Odenwald.

Word of the Boetlingen defeat spread terror everywhere among the insurgents.   The free imperial cities which had come under the heavy hand of the peasants, sighed in relief.   The city of Heilbronn was the first to take steps towards reconciliation with the Suabian Union.   Heilbronn was the seat of the peasants' main office and that of the delegates of the various troops who deliberated over the proposals to be made to the emperor and the empire in the name of all the insurgent peasants.   In these negotiations which were to lay down general rules for all of Germany, it again became apparent that none of the existing estates,

including the peasants, was developed sufficiently to be able
to reconstruct the whole of Germany according to its own
viewpoint. It became obvious that to accomplish this, the
support of the peasantry and particularly of the middle-
class must be gained. In consequence, Wendel Hipler took
over the conduct of the negotiations. Of all the leaders of
the movement, Wendel Hipler had the best understanding
of the existing conditions. He was not a far-seeing revolutionary of Muenzer's type; he was not a representative of
the peasants as were Metzler or Rohrbach; his many-sided
experiences, his practical knowledge of the position of the
various estates towards each other prevented him from
representing one of the estates engaged in the movement
in opposition to the other. Just as Muenzer, a representative of the beginnings of the proletariat then outside of
the existing official organisation of society, was driven to the
anticipation of communism, Wendel Hipler, the representative, as it were, of the average of all progressive elements
of the nation, anticipated modern bourgeois society. The
principles that he defended, the demands that he formulated,
though not immediately possible, were the somewhat ideal-
ised, logical result of the dissolution of feudal society. In
so far as the peasants agreed to propose laws for the whole
empire, they were compelled to accept Hipler's principles
and demands. Centralisation demanded by the peasants
thus assumed, in Heilbronn, a definite form, which, however, was worlds away from the ideas of the peasants themselves on the subject. Centralisation, for instance, was
more clearly defined in the demands for the establishment
of uniform coins, measures and weights, for the abolition
of internal customs, etc., in demands, that is to say, which
were much more in the interests of the city middle-class
than in the interests of the peasants. Concessions made

to the nobility were a certain approach to the modern system of redemption and aimed, finally, to transform feudal land ownership into bourgeois ownership. In a word, so far as the demands of the peasants were combined into a system of "imperial reform," they did not express the temporary demands of the peasants but became subordinate to the general interests of the middle-class as a whole.

While this reform of the empire was still being debated in Heilbronn, the author of the Declaration of the Twelve Articles, Hans Berlin, was already on his way to meet Truchsess, to negotiate in the name of the honourables, the middle-class and the citizenry on the surrender of the city. Reactionary movements within the city supported this betrayal, and Wendel Hipler was obliged to flee, as were the peasants. He went to Weinsberg where he attempted to assemble the remnants of the Wuerttemberg peasants and those few of the Gaildorf troops which could be mobilised. The approach of the Elector Palatine and of Truchsess, however, drove him out of there and he was compelled to go to Wuerzburg to cause the Gay Bright Troop to resume operations. In the meantime, the armies of the Union and the Elector subdued the Neckar region, compelled the peasants to take a new oath, burned many villages, and stabbed or hanged all fleeing peasants that fell into their hands. To avenge the execution of Helfenstein, Weinsberg was burned.

The troops that were assembled in front of Wuerzburg had in the meantime besieged Frauenberg. On May 15, before a gap was made by their fusillade, they bravely but unsuccessfully attempted to storm the fortress. Four hundred of the best men, mostly of Florian Geyer's host, remained in the ditches, dead or wounded. Two days later, May 17, Wendel Hipler appeared and ordered a military council. He proposed to leave at Frauenberg only 4,000 men and to place the main force, about 20,000 men, in a camp at Krautheim on the Jaxt, before the very eyes of Truchsess, so that all reinforcements might be assembled there. The plan was excellent. Only by keeping the masses together, and by a numerical superiority, could one hope to defeat the army of the princes which now numbered about 13,000 men. The demoralisation and discouragement of the peasants, however, had gone too far to make any energetic action possible. Goetz von Berlichingen, who soon afterwards openly appeared as a traitor, may have helped to hold the troop back. Thus Hipler's plan was never put into action; the troops were divided as ever, and only on May 23 did the Gay Bright Troop start action after the Franconians had promised to follow quickly. On May 26, the detachments of the Margrave of Anspach, located in Wuerzburg, were called, due to the word that the Margrave had opened hostilities against the peasants. The rest of the besieging army, with Florian Geyer's Black Troop, took position at Heidingsfeld not far from Wuerzburg.

The Gay Bright Troop arrived on May 24 in Krautheim in a condition far from good. Many peasants learned that in their absence their villages had taken the oath at Truchsess' behest, and this they used as a pretext to go home. The troops moved further to Neckarsulm, and on May 28 started negotiations with Truchsess. At the same time messengers were sent to the peasants of Franconia, Alsace and Black Forest-Hegau, with the demand to hurry reinforcements. From Neckarsulm Goetz marched towards Oehringen. The troops melted from day to day. Goetz von Berlichingen also disappeared during the march. He rode home, having previously negotiated with Truchsess through his old brother-in-arms, Dietrich Spaet, concerning his going over to the other side. In Oehringen, a false rumour of the enemy approaching threw the helpless and discouraged mass into a panic. The troop was rapidly disintegrating, and it was with difficulty that Metzler and Wendel Hipler succeeded in keeping together about 2,000 men, whom they again led towards Krautheim. In the meantime, the Franconian army, 5,000 strong, had come, but in consequence of a side march over Loewenstein towards Oehringen, ordered by Goetz apparently with treacherous intentions, it missed the Gay Troop and moved towards Neckarsulm. This small town, defended by a detachment of the Gay Bright Troop, was besieged by Truchsess. The Franconians arrived at night and saw the fires of the Union army, but their leaders had not the courage to brave an attack. They retreated to Krautheim, where they at last found the remainder of the Gay Bright Troop. Receiving no aid, Neckarsulm surrendered on the 29th to the Union troops. Truchsess immediately ordered 13 peasants executed, and went to meet the troop, burning, pillaging and murdering all along the way through the valleys of Neckar, Kocher and Jaxt. Heaps of ruins and bodies of peasants hanging on trees marked his march.

At Krautheim the Union army met the peasants who, forced by a flank movement of Truchsess, had withdrawn towards Koenigshofen on the Tauber. Here they took their position, 8,000 in number, with 32 cannon. Truchsess approached them, hidden behind hills and forests. He sent out columns to envelop them, and on June 2, he attacked them with such a superiority of forces and energy that in spite of the stubborn resistance of several columns lasting into the night, they were defeated and dispersed. As everywhere, the horsemen of the Union, "the peasants'

death," were mainly instrumental in annihilating the insurgent army, throwing themselves on the peasants, who
were shaken by artillery gun fire and lance attacks, dis-
rupting their ranks completely, and killing individual
fighters.   The kind of warfare conducted by Truchsess and
his horsemen is manifested in the fate of 300 Koenigshof
middle-class men united with the peasant army.   During
the battle, all but fifteen were killed, and of these remaining fifteen, four were subsequently decapitated.

Having thus completed his victory over the peasants of
Odenwald, the Neckar valley and lower Franconia, Truchsess subdued the entire region by means of punitive expeditions, burning entire villages and causing numberless
executions.   From there he moved towards Wuerzburg.   On
his way he learned that the second Franconian troops under
the command of Florian Geyer and Gregor von Burg-Bernsheim was stationed at Sulzdorf.   He immediately moved
against them.

Florian Geyer, who, after the unsuccessful attempt at
storming Frauenberg, had devoted himself mainly to negotiations with the princes and the cities, especially with Rottenburg and Margrave Casimir of Anspach, urging them
to join the peasant fraternity, was suddenly recalled in
consequence of word of the Koenigshofen defeat.   His troops
were joined by those of Anspach under the command of
Gregor von Burg-Bernsheim.   The latter troops had been
only recently formed.   Margrave Casimir had managed, in
true Hohenzollern style, to keep in check the peasant revolt in his region, partly by promises and partly by the
threat of amassing troops.   He maintained complete neutrality towards all outside troops as long as they did not include
Anspach subjects.   He tried to direct the hatred of the
peasants mainly towards the church endowments, through

the ultimate confiscation of which he hoped to enrich himself. As soon as he received word of the Boetlingen battle, he opened hostilities against his rebellious peasants, pillaging and burning their villages, and hanging or otherwise killing many of them. The peasants, however, quickly assembled, and under the command of Gregor von Burg-Bernsheim defeated him at Windsheim, May 29. While they were still pursuing him, the call of the hard-pressed Odenwald peasants reached them, and they turned towards Heidingsfeld and from there with Florian Geyer, again towards Wuerzburg (June 2). Still without word from the Odenwald, they left 5,000 peasants there, and with the remaining 4,000—many had run away—they followed the others. Reassured by false rumours of the outcome of the Koenigshofen battle, they were attacked by Truchsess at Sulzdorf and completely defeated. The horsemen and servants of Truchsess perpetrated, as usual, a terrible massacre. Florian Geyer kept the remainder of his Black Troop, 600 in number, and battled his way through the village of Ingolstadt. He placed 200 men in the church and cemetery and 400 in the castle. He had been pursued by the Elector Palatine's forces, of whom a column of 1,200 men captured the village and set fire to the church. Those who did not perish in the flames were slaughtered. The Elector's troops then fired on the castle, made a gap in the ancient wall, and attempted to storm it. Twice beaten back by the peasants who stood hidden behind an internal wall, they shot the wall to pieces, and attempted a third storming, which was successful. Half of Geyer's men were massacred; with the other 200 he managed to escape. Their hiding place, however, was discovered the following day (Whit-Monday). The Elector Palatine's soldiers surrounded the woods in which they lay hidden, and slaughtered all the men. Only seventeen prisoners were taken during those two days. Florian Geyer again fought his way through with a few of his most intrepid fighters and turned towards the Gaildorf peasants, who had again assembled in a body of about 7,000 men. Upon his arrival, he found them mostly dispersed, in consequence of crushing news from every side. He made a last attempt to assemble the dispersed peasants in the woods on June 9, but was attacked by the troops, and fell fighting.

Truchsess, who, immediately after the Koenigshofen victory, had sent word to the besieged Frauenberg, now marched towards Wuerzburg. The council came to a secret understanding with him so that, on the night of June 7, the Union army was in a position to surround the city where 5,000 peasants were stationed, and the following morning to march through the gates opened by the council, without even lifting a sword. By this betrayal of the Wuerzburg "honourables" the last troops of the Franconian peasants were disarmed and all the leaders arrested. Truchsess immediately ordered 81 of them decapitated. Here in Wuerzburg the various Franconian princes appeared, one after the other, among them the Bishop of Wuerzburg himself, the Bishop of Bamberg and the Margrave of Brandenburg-Anspach. The gracious lords distributed the rôles among themselves. Truchsess marched with the Bishop of Bamberg, who presently broke the agreement concluded with his peasants and offered his territory to the raging hordes of the Union army, who pillaged, massacred and burned. Margrave Casimir devastated his own land. Teiningen was burned, numerous villages were pillaged or made fuel for the flames. In every city the Margrave held a bloody court. In Neustadt, on the Aisch, he ordered eighteen rebels beheaded, in the Buergel March, forty-three

suffered a similar fate. From there he went to Rottenburg
where the honourables, in the meantime, had made a counter
revolution and arrested Stephan von Menzingen. The
Rottenburg lower middle-class and plebeians were now compelled to pay heavily for the fact that they behaved towards
the peasants in such an equivocal way, refusing to help
them to the very last moment and in their local narrow-
minded egotism insisting on the suppression of the countryside crafts in favour of the city guilds, and only unwillingly
renouncing the city revenues flowing from the feudal
services of the peasants. The Margrave ordered sixteen of them executed, Menzingen among them. In a
similar manner the Bishop of Wuerzburg marched through
his region, pillaging, devastating and burning everywhere.
On his triumphal march he ordered 256 rebels to be decapitated, and upon his return to Wuerzburg he crowned his
work by decapitating thirteen more from among the Wuerzburg rebels.

In the region of Mainz the viceroy, Bishop Wilhelm von
Strassburg, restored order without resistance. He ordered
only four men executed. Rheingau, where the peasants had
also been restless, but where, nevertheless, everybody had
long before gone home, was subsequently invaded by Frowen
von Hutten, a cousin of Ulrich, and finally "pacified" by
the execution of twelve ringleaders. Frankfurt, which also
had witnessed revolutionary movements of a considerable
size, was held in check first by the conciliatory attitude of
the council, then by recruited troops in the Rhenish Palatinate. Eight thousand peasants had assembled anew after
the breach of agreement by the Elector, and had again
burned monasteries and castles, but the Archbishop of Trier
came to the aid of the Marshal of Zabern, and defeated
them as early as May 23 at Pfedersheim. A series of

atrocities (in Pfedersheim alone eighty-two were executed) and the capture of Weissenburg on July 7 terminated the insurrection here.

Of all the divisions of troops there remained only two to be vanquished, those of Hegau-Black Forest and of Allgaeu.   Archduke Ferdinand had tried intrigues with both.   In the same way as Margrave Casimir and other princes tried to utilise the insurrection to annex the church territories and principalities, so Ferdinand wished to utilise it to strengthen the power of the House of Austria.   He had negotiated with the Allgaeu commander, Walter Bach, and with the Hegau commander, Hans Mueller, with the aim of inducing the peasants to declare their adherence to Austria, but, both chiefs being venal, their influence with the troops went only so far that the Allgaeu troop concluded an armistice with the Archbishop and observed neutrality towards Austria.

Retreating from the Wuerttemberg region, the peasants of Hegau destroyed a number of castles, and received reinforcements from the provinces of the Margraviate of Baden. On May 13 they marched towards Freiburg; on May 18 they bombarded it, and on May 23, the city having capitulated, they entered it with flying colours.   From there they moved towards Stockach and Radolfzell, and waged a prolonged petty war against the garrisons of those cities.   The latter, together with the nobility and other surrounding cities, appealed to the Lake peasants for help in accordance with the Weingarten agreement.   The former rebels of the Lake Troop rose, 5,000 strong, against their former allies. So potent was the narrow-mindedness of the peasants who were confined to their local horizon, that only 600 refused to fight and expressed a desire to join the Hegau peasants, for which they were slaughtered.   The Hegau peasants, themselves, persuaded by Hans Mueller of Bulgenbach, who had sold himself to the enemy, lifted their siege, and Hans Mueller having run away, most of them dispersed forthwith. The remaining ones entrenched themselves on the Hilzingen Steep, where, on July 16, they were beaten and annihilated by the troops that had in the meantime become free of other engagements. The Swiss cities negotiated an agreement with the Hegau peasants, which, however, did not prevent the other side from capturing and murdering Hans Mueller, his Laufenburg betrayal notwithstanding. In Breisgau, the city of Freiburg also deserted the peasant Union (July 17) and sent troops against it, but because of the weakness of the fighting forces of the princes, here as elsewhere, an agreement was reached (September 18), which also included Sundgau. The eight groups of the Black Forest and the Klettgau peasants, who were not yet disarmed, were again driven to an uprising by the tyranny of Count von Sulz, and were repulsed in October. On November 13, the Black Forest peasants were forced into an agreement, and on December 6, Walzhut, the last bulwark of the insurrection in the Upper Rhine, fell.

The Allgaeu peasants had, after the departure of Truchsess, renewed their campaign against the monasteries and castles and were using repressive measures in retaliation for the devastations caused by the Union army. They were confronted by few troops which braved only insignificant skirmishes, not being able to follow them into the woods. In June, a movement against the honourables started in Memmingen which had hitherto remained more or less neutral, and only the accidental nearness of some Union troops which came in time to the rescue of the nobility, made its suppression possible. Schapelar, the preacher and leader of the plebeian movement, fled to St.

Gallen. The peasants appeared before the city and were about to start firing to break a gap, when they learned of the approach of Truchsess on his way from Wuerzburg. On June 27 they started against him, in two columns, over Babenhausen and Oberguenzburg. Archduke Ferdinand again attempted to win over the peasants to the House of Austria. Citing the armistice concluded with the peasants, he demanded of Truchsess to march no further against them. The Suabian Union, however, ordered Truchsess to attack them, but to refrain from pillaging and burning. Truchsess, however, was too clever to relinquish his primary and most effective means of battle, even were he in a position to keep in order the Lansquenets whom he had led between Lake Constance and the Main from one excess to another. The peasants took a stand behind the Iller and the Luibas, about 23,000 in number. Truchsess opposed them with 11,000. The positions of both armies were formidable. The cavalry could not operate on the territory that lay ahead, and if the Truchsess Lansquenets were superior to the peasants in organisation, military resources and discipline, the Allgaeu peasants counted in their ranks a host of former soldiers and experienced commanders and possessed numerous well-manned cannon. On July 19, the armies of the Suabian Union opened a cannonade which was continued on every side on the 20th, but without result. On July 21, Georg von Frundsberg joined Truchsess with 300 Lansquenets. He knew many of the peasant commanders who had served under him in the Italian military expeditions and he entered into negotiations with them. Where military resources were insufficient, treason succeeded. Walter Bach and several other commanders and artillerymen sold themselves. They set fire to the powder store of the peasants and persuaded the troops to make an enveloping movement, but as soon as the peasants left their strong position they fell into the ambush placed by Truchsess in collusion with Bach and the other traitors. They were less capable of defending themselves since their traitorous commanders had left them under the pretext of reconnoitering and were already on their way to Switzerland. Thus two of the peasant camps were entirely disrupted. The third, under Knopf of Luibas, was still in a position to withdraw in order. It again took its position on the mountain of Kollen near Kampten, where it was surrounded by Truchsess. The latter did not dare to attack these peasants, but he cut them off from all supplies, and tried to demoralise them by burning about 200 villages in the vicinity. Hunger, and the sight of their burning homes, finally brought the peasants to surrender (July 25). More than twenty were immediately executed. Knopf of Luibas, the only leader of this troop who did not betray his banner, fled to Biegenz. There he was captured, however, and hanged, after a long imprisonment.

With this, the Peasant War in Suabia and Franconia came to an end.

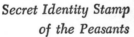

Secret Identity Stamp of the Peasants

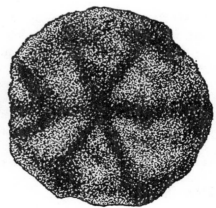

CHAPTER VI

IMMEDIATELY after the outbreak of the first movement in Suabia, Thomas Muenzer again hurried to Thuringia, and since the end of February and the beginning of March, he established his quarters in the free imperial city of Muehlhausen, where his party was stronger than elsewhere. He held the threads of the entire movement in his hand. He knew what storm was about to break in Southern Germany, and he undertook to make Thuringia the centre of the movement for North Germany. He found very fertile soil. Thuringia, the main arena of the Reformation movement, was in the grip of great unrest. The economic misery of the downtrodden peasants, as well as the current revolutionary, religious and political doctrine, had also prepared the neighbouring provinces, Hesse, Saxony, and the region of the Harz, for the general uprising. In Muehlhausen itself, whole masses of the lower middle-class had been won over to the extreme Muenzer doctrine, and could hardly wait for the moment when they would assert themselves by a superiority of numbers against the haughty honourables. In order not to start before the proper moment, Muenzer was compelled to appear in the rôle of moderator, but his disciple, Pfeifer, who conducted the movement there, had committed himself to such an extent that he could not hold back the outbreak, and as early as March 17, 1525, before the general uprising in Southern Germany, Muehlhausen had its revolution. The old patrician council

134

was overthrown, and the government was handed over to the newly-elected "eternal council," with Muenzer as president.

The worst thing that can befall a leader of an extreme party is to be compelled to take over a government in an epoch when the movement is not yet ripe for the domination of the class which he represents and for the realisation of the measures which that domination would imply. What he *can* do depends not upon his will but upon the sharpness of the clash of interests between the various classes, and upon the degree of development of the material means of existence, the relations of production and means of communication upon which the clash of interests of the classes is based every time. What he *ought* to do, what his party demands of him, again depends not upon him, or upon the degree of development of the class struggle and its conditions. He is bound to his doctrines and the demands hitherto propounded which do not emanate from the interrelations of the social classes at a given moment, or from the more or less accidental level of relations of production and means of communication, but from his more or less penetrating insight into the general result of the social and political movement. Thus he necessarily finds himself in a dilemma. What he *can* do is in contrast to all his actions as hitherto practised, to all his principles and to the present interests of his party; what he *ought* to do cannot be achieved. In a word, he is compelled to represent not his party or his class, but the class for whom conditions are ripe for domination. In the interests of the movement itself, he is compelled to defend the interests of an alien class, and to feed his own class with phrases and promises, with the assertion that the interests of that alien class are their own interests. Whoever puts himself in this awkward position is irrevocably lost. We have seen examples of this in recent times. We need only be reminded of the position taken in the last French provisional government by the representatives of the proletariat, though they represented only a very low level of proletarian development. Whoever can still look forward to official positions after having become familiar with the experiences of the February government—not to speak of our own noble German provisional governments and imperial regencies—is either foolish beyond measure, or at best pays only lip service to the extreme revolutionary party.

Muenzer's position at the head of the "eternal council" of Muehlhausen was indeed much more precarious than that of any modern revolutionary regent. Not only the movement of his time, but the whole century, was not ripe for the realisation of the ideas for which he himself had only begun to grope. The class which he represented not only was not developed enough and incapable of subduing and transforming the whole of society, but it was just beginning to come into existence. The social transformation that he pictured in his fantasy was so little grounded in the then existing economic conditions that the latter were a preparation for a social system diametrically opposed to that of which he dreamt. Nevertheless, he was bound to his preachings of Christian equality and evangelical community of possessions. He was at least compelled to make an attempt at their realisation. Community of all possessions, universal and equal labour duty, and the abolition of all authority were proclaimed. In reality, Muehlhausen remained a republican imperial city with a somewhat democratic constitution, with a senate elected by universal suffrage and under the control of a forum, and with the hastily improvised feeding of the poor. The social change, which so horrified the Protestant middle-class contemporaries, in reality never went beyond a feeble and unconscious attempt prematurely to establish the bourgeois society of a later period.

Muenzer, himself, seems to have realised the wide abyss between his theories and surrounding realities. This abyss must have been felt the more keenly, the more distorted the views of this genius of necessity appeared, reflected in the heads of the mass of his followers. He threw himself into widening and organising the movement with a zeal rare even for him. He wrote letters and sent out emissaries in all directions. His letters and sermons breathed a revolutionary fanaticism which was amazing in comparison with his former writings. Gone completely was the naïve youthful humour of Muenzer's revolutionary pamphlets. The quiet instructive language of the thinker, which had been so characteristic of him, appeared no more. Muenzer was now entirely a prophet of the revolution. Incessantly he fanned the flame of hatred against the ruling classes. He spurred the wildest passions, using forceful terms of expression the like of which religious and nationalist delirium had put into the mouths of the Old Testament prophets. The style up to which he worked himself reveals the level of education of that public which he was to affect. The example of Muehlhausen and the propaganda of Muenzer had a quick and far-reaching effect. In Thuringia, Eichsfeld, Harz, in the duchies of Saxony, in Hesse and Fulda, in Upper Franconia and in Vogtland, the peasants arose, assembled in armies, and burned castles and monasteries. Muenzer was more or less recognised as the leader of the entire movement, and Muehlhausen remained the central point, while in Erfurt a purely middle-class movement became victorious, and the ruling party there constantly maintained an undecided attitude towards the peasants.

In Thuringia, the princes were at the beginning just as helpless and powerless in relation to the peasants as they had been in Franconia and Suabia. Only in the last days of April, did the Landgrave of Hesse succeed in assembling a corps. It was that same Landgrave Philipp, whose piety is being praised so much by the Protestant and bourgeois histories of the Reformation, and of whose infamies towards the peasants we will presently have a word to say. By a series of quick movements and by decisive action, Landgrave Philipp subdued the major part of his land. He called new contingents, and then turned towards the region of the Abbot of Fulda, who hitherto was his lord. On May 3, he defeated the Fulda peasant troop at Frauenberg, subdued the entire land, and seized the opportunity not only to free himself from the sovereignty of the Abbot, but to make the Abbey of Fulda a vassalage of Hesse, naturally pending its subsequent secularisation. He then took Eisenach and Langensalza, and jointly with the Saxon troops, moved towards the headquarters of the rebellious Muehlhausen. Muenzer assembled his forces at Frankenhausen 8,000 men and several cannons. The Thuringian troops were far from possessing that fighting power which the Suabian and Franconian troops developed in their struggle with Truchsess. The men were poorly armed and badly disciplined. They counted few ex-soldiers among them, and sorely lacked leadership. It appears that Muenzer possessed no military knowledge whatsoever. Nevertheless, the princes found it proper to use here the same tactics that so often helped Truchsess to victory—breach of faith. On May 16, they entered negotiations, concluded an armistice, but attacked the peasants before the time of the armistice had elapsed.

Muenzer stood with his people on the mountain which is still called Mount Battle (Schlachtberg), entrenched behind a barricade of wagons. The discouragement among the troops was rapidly increasing. The princes had promised them amnesty should they deliver Muenzer alive. Muenzer assembled his people in a circle, to debate the princes' proposals. A knight and a priest expressed themselves in favour of capitulation. Muenzer had them both brought inside the circle, and decapitated. This act of terrorist energy, jubilantly met by the outspoken revolutionaries, caused a certain halt among the troops, but most of the men would have gone away without resistance had it not been noticed that the princes' Lansquenets, who had encircled the entire mountain, were approaching in close columns, in spite of the armistice. A front was hurriedly formed behind the wagons, but already the cannon balls and guns were pounding the half-defenseless peasants, unused to battle, and the Lansquenets reached the barricade. After a brief resistance, the line of the wagons was broken, the peasants' cannon captured, and the peasants dispersed. They fled in wild disorder, and fell into the hands of the enveloping columns and the cavalry, who perpetrated an appalling massacre among them. Out of 8,000 peasants, over 5,000 were slaughtered. The survivors arrived at Frankenhaus, and simultaneously with them, the princes' cavalry. The city was taken. Muenzer, wounded in the head, was discovered in a house and captured. On May 25, Muehlhausen also surrendered. Pfeifer, who had remained there, ran away, but was captured in the region of Eisenach.

Muenzer was put on the rack in the presence of the

princes, and then decapitated. He went to his death with
the same courage with which he had lived. He was barely
twenty-eight when he was executed. Pfeifer, with many
others, was also executed. In Fulda, that holy man,
Philipp of Hesse, had opened his bloody court. He and
the Prince of Hesse ordered many others to be killed by
the sword—in Eisenach, twenty-four; in Langensalza, forty-
one; after the battle of Frankenhaus, 300; in Muehlhausen,
over 100; at Germar, twenty-six; at Tungeda, fifty, at
Sangenhausen, twelve; in Leipzig, eight, not to speak of
mutilations and the more moderate measures of pillaging
and burning villages and cities.

Muehlhausen was compelled to give up its liberty under
the empire, and was incorporated into the Saxon lands,
just as the Abbey of Fulda was incorporated in the Land-
graviate of Hesse.

The prince now moved through the forest of Thuringia,
where Franconian peasants of the Bildhaus camp had united
with the Thuringians, and burned many castles. A battle
took place before Meiningen. The peasants were beaten
and withdrew towards the city, which closed its gates to
them, and threatened to attack them from the rear. The
troops, thus placed in a quandary by the betrayal of their
allies, capitulated before the prince, and dispersed, while
negotiations were still under way. The camp of Bildhaus
had long dispersed, and with this, the remnants of the
insurgents of Saxony, Hesse, Thuringia and Upper Franconia, were annihilated.

In Alsace the rebellion broke out after the movement had
started on the right side of the Rhine. The peasants of the
bishopric of Strassbourg arose as late as the middle of April.
Soon after, there was an upheaval of the peasants of Upper
Alsace and Sundgau. On April 18, a contingent of Lower

Alsace peasants pillaged the monastery of Altdorf. Other troops were formed near Ebersheim and Barr, as well as in the Urbis valley. These were soon concentrated into the large Lower Alsace division and proceeded in an organised way to take cities and towns and to destroy monasteries. One out of every three men was called to the colours. The Twelve Articles of this group were considerably more radical than those of the Suabian and Franconian groups.

While one column of the Lower Alsace peasants first concentrated near St. Hippolite early in May, attempting to take the city but without success, and then, through an understanding with the citizens, came into possession of Barken on May 10, of Rappoldtsweiler on May 13, and Reichenweier on May 14, a second column under Erasmus Gerber marched to attack Strassbourg by surprise. The attempt was unsuccessful, and the column now turned towards the Vosges, destroyed the monastery of Mauersmuenster, and besieged Zabern, taking it on May 13. From here it moved towards the frontier of Lorraine and aroused the section of the duchy adjoining the frontier, at the same time fortifying the mountain passes. Two columns were formed at Herbolzheim on the Saar, and at Neuburg, at Saargemund, 4,000 German-Lorraine peasants entrenched themselves. Finally, two advanced troops, the Kolben in the Vosges at Stuerzelbrunn, and the Kleeburg at Weissenburg, covered the front and the right flank, while the left flank was adjoining those of Upper Alsace.

The latter, in motion since April 20, had forced the city of Sulz into the peasant fraternity on May 10, Gebweiler, on May 12, and Sennheim and vicinity, May 15. The Austrian government and the surrounding imperial cities immediately united against them, but they were too weak to offer serious resistance, not to speak of attack. Thus, in the middle of May, the whole of Alsace, with the exception of only a few cities, came into the hands of the insurgents.

But already the army was approaching which was destined to break the ungodly attack of the Alsace peasants. It was the French who effected here the restoration of the nobility. Already, on May 16, Duke Anton of Lorraine marched out with an army of 30,000, among them the flower of the French nobility, as well as Spanish, Piedmontese, Lombardic, Greek and Albanian auxiliary troops. On May 16 he met 4,000 peasants at Luetzelstein whom he defeated without effort, and on the 17th he forced Zabern, which was besieged by the peasants, to surrender. But even while the Lorrainers were entering the city and the peasants were being disarmed, the conditions of the surrender were broken. The defenseless peasants were attacked by the Lansquenets and most of them were slaughtered. The remaining Lower Alsace columns disbanded, and Duke Anton went to meet the Upper Alsatians. The latter, who had refused to join the Lower Alsatians at Zabern, were now attacked at Scherweiler by the entire force of the Lorrainers. They resisted with great bravery, but the enormous numerical superiority—30,000 as against 7,000—and the betrayal of a number of knights, especially that of the magistrate of Reichenweier, made all daring futile. They were totally beaten and dispersed. The Duke subdued the whole of Alsace with the usual atrocities. Only Sundgau was spared. By threatening to call him into the land, the Austrian government forced the peasants to conclude the Ensisheim agreement early in June. The government soon broke the agreement, however, ordering numbers of preachers and leaders of the movement to be hanged. The peasants made a new insurrection which ended with the inclusion of the Sundgau peasants into the Offenburg agreement (September 18).

There now remains only the report of the Peasant War in the Alpine regions of Austria. These regions, as well as the adjoining Archbishopric of Salzburg were in continuous opposition to the government and the nobility ever since the Stara Prawa, and the Reformation doctrines found there a fertile soil. Religious persecutions and wilful taxation brought the rebellion to a crisis.

The city of Salzburg, supported by the peasants and the pitmen, had been in controversy with the Archbishop since 1522 over city privileges and the freedom of religious practice. By the end of 1523, the Archbishop attacked the city with recruited Lansquenets, terrorised it by a cannonade from the castle, and persecuted the heretical preachers. At the same time he imposed new crushing taxes, and thereby irritated the population to the utmost. In the spring of 1525, simultaneously with the Suabian-Franconian and Thuringian uprisings, the peasants and pitmen of the entire country suddenly arose, organised themselves under the commanders Brossler and Weitmoser, freed the city and besieged the castle of Salzburg. Like the West German peasants, they organised a Christian alliance and formulated their demands into fourteen articles.

In Styria, in Upper Austria, in Carinthia and Carniola, where new extortionate taxes, duties and edicts had severely injured the interests closest to the people, the peasants arose in the Spring of 1525. They took a number of castles and at Grys, defeated the conqueror of the Stara Prawa, the old field commander Dietrichstein. Although the government succeeded in placating some of the insurgents with false promises, the bulk of them remained together and united with the Salzburg peasants, so that the entire region of

Salzburg and the major part of Upper Austria, Styria, Carinthia and Carniola were in the hands of the peasants and pitmen.

In the Tyrol, the Reformation doctrines had also found adherence. Here even more than in the other Alpine regions of Austria, Muenzer's emissaries had been successfully active. Archbishop Ferdinand persecuted the preachers of the new doctrines here as elsewhere, and impinged the rights of the population by arbitrary financial regulations. In consequence, an uprising took place in the Spring of 1525. The insurgents, whose commander was a Muenzer man named Geismaier, the only noted military talent among all the peasant chiefs, took a great number of castles, and proceeded energetically against the priests, particularly in the south and the region of Etsch. The Vorarlberg peasants also arose and joined the Allgaeu peasants.

The Archbishop, pressed from every side, now began to make concession after concession to the rebels whom a short time before he had wished to annihilate by means of burning, scourging, pillaging and murdering. He summoned the Diets of the hereditary lands, and pending their assembling, concluded an armistice with the peasants. In the meantime he was strenuously arming, in order, as soon as possible, to be able to speak to the ungodly ones in a different language.

Naturally, the armistice was not kept long. Dietrichstein, having run short of cash, began to levy contributions in the duchies; his Slavic and Magyar troops allowed themselves, besides, the most shameful atrocities against the population. This brought the Styrians to new rebellion. The peasants attacked Dietrichstein at Schladming during the night of July 3d and slaughtered everybody who did not speak German. Dietrichstein himself was captured.

On the morning of July 4, the peasants organised a jury to try the captives, and forty Czech and Croatian noble prisoners were sentenced to death. This was effective. The Archbishop immediately consented to all the demands of the estates of the five duchies (Upper and Lower Austria, Styria, Carinthia and Carniola).

In Tyrol, the demands of the Diet were also granted, and thereby the North was quieted. The South, however, insisting on its original demands as against the much more moderate decisions of the Diet, remained under arms. Only in December was the Archbishop in a position to restore order by force. He did not fail to execute a great number of instigators and leaders of the upheaval who fell into his hands.

Now 10,000 Bavarians moved against Salzburg, under Georg of Frundsberg. This imposing military power, as well as the quarrels that had broken out among the peasants, induced the Salzburg peasants to conclude an agreement with the Archbishop, which came into being September 1, and was also accepted by the Archduke. In spite of this, the two princes, who had meanwhile considerably strengthened their troops, soon broke the agreement and thereby drove the Salzburg peasants to a new uprising. The insurgents held their own throughout the winter. In the Spring, Geismaier came to them to open a splendid campaign against the troops which were approaching from every side. In a series of brilliant battles in May and June, 1526, he defeated the Bavarian, Austrian and Suabian Union troops and the Lansquenets of the Archbishop of Salzburg, one after another, and for a long time he prevented the various corps from uniting. He also found time to besiege Radstadt. Finally, surrounded by overwhelming forces, he was compelled to withdraw. He battled his way through and led the remnants of his corps through the Austrian Alps into Venetian territory. The republic of Venice and Switzerland offered the indefatigable peasant chief starting points for new conspiracies. For a whole year he was still attempting to involve them in a war against Austria, which would have offered him an occasion for a new peasant uprising. The hand of the murderer, however, reached him in the course of these negotiations. Archbishop Ferdinand and the Archbishop of Salzburg could not rest as long as Geismaier was alive. They therefore paid a bandit who, in 1527, succeeded in removing the dangerous rebel from among the living.

REVENGE OF THE PRINCES

Trial, Sentence and Execution

CHAPTER VII

AFTER Geismaier's withdrawal into Venetian territory, the epilogue of the Peasant War was ended. The peasants were everywhere brought again under the sway of their ecclesiastical, noble or patrician masters. The agreements that were concluded with them here and there were broken, and heavy burdens were augmented by the enormous indemnities imposed by the victors on the vanquished. The magnificent attempt of the German people ended in ignominious defeat and, for a time, in greater oppression. In the long run, however, the situation of the peasants did not become worse. Whatever the nobility, princes and priests could wring out of the peasants had been wrung out even before the war. The German peasant of that time had this in common with the modern proletarian, that his share in the products of the work was limited to a subsistence minimum necessary for his maintenance and for the propagation of the race. It is true that peasants of some little wealth were ruined. Hosts of bondsmen were forced into serfdom; whole stretches of community lands were confiscated; a great number of peasants were driven into vagabondage or forced to become city plebeians by the destruction of their domiciles and the devastation of their fields in addition to the general disorder. Wars and devastations, however, were every-day phenomena at that time, and in general, the peasant class was on too low a level to have its situation made worse for a long time through increased taxes. The subsequent religious wars and finally the Thirty Years' War with its con-

147

stantly repeated mass devastations and depopulations pounded the peasants much more painfully than did the Peasant War. It was notably the Thirty Years' War which annihilated the most important parts of the productive forces in agriculture, through which, as well as through the simultaneous destruction of many cities, it lowered the living standards of the peasants, plebeians and the ruined city inhabitants to the level of Irish misery in its worst form.

The class that suffered most from the Peasant War was the *clergy*. Its monasteries and endowments were burned down; its valuables plundered, sold into foreign countries, or melted; its stores of goods consumed. They had been, least of all capable of offering resistance, and at the same time the weight of the people's old hatred fell heaviest upon them. The other estates, princes, nobility and the middle-class, even experienced a secret joy at the sufferings of the hated prelates. The Peasant War had made popular the secularisation of the church estates in favour of the peasants. The lay princes, and to a certain degree the cities, determined to bring about secularisation in their own interests, and soon the possessions of the prelates in Protestant countries were in the hands of either the princes or the honourables. The power and authority of the ecclesiastical princes were also infringed upon, and the lay princes understood how to exploit the people's hatred also in this direction. Thus we have seen how the Abbot of Fulda was relegated from a feudal lord of Philipp of Hesse to the position of his vassal. Thus the city of Kempten forced the ecclesiastical prince to sell to it for a trifle a series of precious privileges which he enjoyed in the city.

The *nobility* had also suffered considerably. Most of its castles were destroyed, and a number of its most respected families were ruined and could find means of subsistence only in the service of the princes. Its power-lessness in relation to the peasants was proven. It had been beaten everywhere and forced to surrender. Only the armies of the princes had saved it. The nobility was bound more and more to lose its significance as a free estate under the empire and to fall under the dominion of the princes.

Nor did the *cities* generally gain any advantages from the Peasant War. The rule of the honourables was almost everywhere reestablished with new force, and the opposi-tion of the middle-class remained broken for a long time. Old patrician routine thus dragged on, hampering commerce and industry in every way, up to the French Revolution. Moreover, the cities were made responsible by the princes for the momentary successes which the middle-class or plebeian parties had achieved within their confines during the struggle. Cities which had previously belonged to the princes were forced to pay heavy indemnities, robbed of their privileges, and made subject to the avaricious wilful-ness of the princes (Frankenhausen, Arnstadt, Schmal-kalden, Wurzburg, etc.), cities of the empire were incor-porated into territories of the princes (Muehlhausen), or they were at least placed under moral dependence on the princes of the adjoining territory, as was the case with many imperial cities in Franconia.

The sole gainers under these conditions were the *princes*. We have seen at the beginning of our exposition that low development of industry, commerce and agriculture made the centralisation of the Germans into a *nation* impossible, that it allowed only local and provincial centralisation, and that the princes, representing centralisation within disrup-tion, were the only class to profit from every change in the existing social and political conditions. The state of development of Germany in those days was so low and at the same time so different in various provinces, that along with lay principalities there could still exist ecclesiastical sovereignties, city republics, and sovereign counts and barons. Simultaneously, however, this development was continually, though slowly and feebly, pressing towards *provincial* centralisation, towards subjugating all imperial estates under the princes. It is due to this that only the princes could gain by the ending of the Peasant War. This happened in reality. They gained not only relatively, through the weakening of their opponents, the clergy, the nobility and the cities, but also absolutely through the prizes of war which they collected. The church estates were secularised in their favour; part of the nobility, fully or partly ruined, was obliged gradually to place itself in their vassalage; the indemnities of the cities and peasantry swelled their treasuries, which, with the abolition of so many city privileges, had now obtained a much more extended field for financial operations.

The decentralisation of Germany, the widening and strengthening of which was the chief result of the war, was at the same time the cause of its failure.

We have seen that Germany was split not only into numberless independent provinces almost totally foreign to each other, but that in every one of these provinces the nation was divided into various strata of estates and parts of estates. Besides princes and priests we find nobility and peasants in the countryside; patricians, middle-class and plebeians in the cities. At best, these classes were indifferent to each other's interests if not in actual conflict. Above all these complicated interests there still were the interests of the empire and the pope. We have seen that, with great difficulty, imperfectly, and differing in various localities, these various interests finally formed three great groups. We have seen that in spite of this grouping, achieved with so much labour, every estate opposed the line indicated by circumstances for the national development, every estate conducting the movement of its own accord, coming into conflict not only with the conservatives but also with the rest of the opposition estates. Failure was, therefore, inevitable. This was the fate of the nobility in Sickingen's uprising, the fate of the peasants in the Peasant War, of the middle-class in their tame Reformation. This was the fate even of the peasants and plebeians who in most localities of Germany could not unite for common action and stood in each other's way. We have also seen the causes of this split in the class struggle and the resultant defeat of the middle-class movement.

How local and provincial decentralisation and the resultant local and provincial narrow-mindedness ruined the whole movement, how neither middle-class nor peasantry nor plebeians could unite for concerted national action; how the peasants of every province acted only for themselves, as a rule refusing aid to the insurgent peasants of the neighbouring region, and therefore being annihilated in individual battles one after another by armies which in most cases counted hardly one-tenth of the total number of the insurgent masses,—all this must be quite clear to the reader from this presentation. The armistices and the agreements concluded by individual groups with their enemies also constituted acts of betrayal of the common cause, and the grouping of the various troops not according to the greater or smaller community of their own actions, the only possible grouping, but according to the community of the special adversary to whom they succumbed, is striking proof of the degree of the mutual alienation of the peasants in various provinces.

The analogy with the movement of 1848-50 is here also apparent. In 1848 as in the Peasant War, the interests of the opposition classes clashed with each other and each acted of its own accord. The bourgeoisie, developed sufficiently not to tolerate any longer the feudal and bureaucratic absolutism, was not powerful enough to subordinate the claims of other classes to its own interests. The proletariat, too weak to be able to count on skipping the bourgeois period and immediately conquering power for itself, had, still under absolutism, tasted too well the sweetness of bourgeois government, and was generally far too developed to identify for one moment its own emancipation with the emancipation of the bourgeoisie. The mass of the nation, small bourgeois artisans and peasants, were left in the lurch by their nearest and natural allies, the bourgeoisie, because they were too revolutionary, and partly by the proletariat because they were not sufficiently advanced. Divided in itself, this mass of the nation achieved nothing, while opposing their fellow opponents on the right and the left. As to provincial narrow-mindedness, it could hardly have been greater in 1525 among the peasants than it was among the classes participating in the movement of 1848. The hundred local revolutions as well as the hundred local reactions following them and completed without hindrance, the retention of the split into numerous small states—all this speaks loud enough indeed. *He who, after the two German revolutions, of 1525 and 1548, and their results, still dreams of a federated republic, belongs in a house for the insane.*

Still, the two revolutions, that of the Sixteenth Century and that of 1848-50, are, in spite of all analogies, materially different from each other. The revolution of 1848 bespeaks, if not the progress of Germany, the progress of Europe.

Who profited by the revolution of 1525? The princes. Who profited by the revolution of 1848? The *big* princes, Austria and Prussia. Behind the princes of 1525 there stood the lower middle-class of the cities, held chained by means of taxation. Behind the big provinces of 1850, there stood the modern big bourgeoisie, quickly subjugating them by means of the State debt. Behind the big bourgeoisie stand the proletarians.

The revolution of 1525 was a local German affair. The English, French, Bohemians and Hungarians had already gone through their peasant wars when the Germans began theirs. If Germany was decentralised, Europe was so to a much greater extent. The revolution of 1848 was not a local German affair, it was one phase of a great European movement. The moving forces throughout the period of its duration were not confined to the narrow limits of one individual country, not even to the limits of one-quarter of the globe. In fact, the countries which were the arena of the revolution were least active in producing it. They were more or less unconscious raw materials without a will of their own. They were moulded in the course of a movement in which the entire world participated, a movement which under existing social conditions may appear to us as an alien power, but which, in the end, is nothing but our own. This is why the revolution of 1848-50 could not end in the way that the revolution of 1525 ended.

THE END

THE TWELVE ARTICLES OF THE PEASANTS

Handlung / Articfel / vnnd Instruction / so fürgenõ
men woïden sein vonn allen Rottenn vnnõ
hauffen der Pauren / so sichßesamen
verpflicht haben: M: D:xxv:

TITLE PAGE OF THE
TWELVE ARTICLES

THE TWELVE ARTICLES OF THE PEASANTS *

THE fundamental and correct chief articles of all the peasants and of those subject to ecclesiastical lords, relating to these matters in which they feel themselves aggrieved.

M cccc, quadratum, lx et duplicatum
V cum transibit, christiana secta peribit.

Peace to the Christian Reader and the Grace of God through Christ.

There are many evil writings put forth of late which take occasion, on account of the assembling of the peasants, to cast scorn upon the gospel, saying: Is this the fruit of the new teaching, that no one should obey but all should everywhere rise in revolt and rush together to reform or perhaps destroy altogether the authorities, both ecclesiastic and lay? The articles below shall answer these godless and criminal fault-finders, and serve in the first place to remove the reproach from the word of God, and in the second place to give a Christian excuse for the disobedience or even the revolt of the entire Peasantry. In the first place the Gospel is not the cause of revolt and disorder, since it is the message of Christ, the promised Messiah, the Word of Life, teaching only love, peace, patience and

* *Translations and Reprints from the Original Sources of European History*, Vol. II, published by the Department of History, University of Pennsylvania.

concord. Thus, all who believe in Christ should learn to be loving, peaceful, long-suffering and harmonious. This is the foundation of all the articles of the peasants (as will be seen) who accept the Gospel and live according to it. How then can the evil reports declare the Gospel to be a cause of revolt and disobedience? That the authors of the evil reports and the enemies of the Gospel oppose themselves to these demands is due, not to the Gospel, but to the Devil, the worst enemy of the Gospel, who causes this opposition by raising doubts in the minds of his followers, and thus the word of God, which teaches love, peace and concord, is overcome. In the second place, it is clear that the peasants demand that this Gospel be taught them as a guide in life and they ought not to be called disobedient or disorderly. Whether God grant the peasants (earnestly wishing to live according to His word) their requests or no, who shall find fault with the will of the Most High? Who shall meddle in His judgments or oppose his majesty? Did he not hear the children of Israel when they called upon Him and saved them out of the hands of Pharaoh? Can He not save His own to-day? Yes, He will save them and that speedily. Therefore, Christian reader, read the following articles with care and then judge. Here follow the articles:

The First Article.—First, it is our humble petition and desire, as also our will and resolution, that in the future we should have power and authority so that each community should choose and appoint a pastor, and that we should have the right to depose him should he conduct himself improperly. The pastor thus chosen should teach us the Gospel pure and simple, without any addition, doctrine or ordinance of man. For to teach us continually the true faith will lead us to pray God that through His grace this faith may increase within us and become part of us. For if His grace work not within us we remain flesh and blood, which availeth nothing; since the Scripture clearly teaches that only through true faith can we come to God. Only through His mercy can we become holy. Hence such a guide and pastor is necessary and in this fashion grounded upon the Scriptures.

The Second Article.—According as the just tithe is established by the Old Testament and fulfilled in the New, we are ready and willing to pay the fair tithe of grain. The word of God plainly provided that in giving according to right to God and distributing to His people the services of a pastor are required. We will that, for the future, our church provost, whomsoever the community may appoint, shall gather and receive this tithe. From this he shall give to the pastor, elected by the whole community, a decent and sufficient maintenance for him and his, as shall seem right to the whole community (or, with the knowledge of the community). What remains over shall be given to the poor of the place, as the circumstances and the general opinion demand. Should anything farther remain, let it be kept, lest any one should have to leave the country from poverty. Provision should also be made from this surplus to avoid laying any land tax on the poor. In case one or more villages themselves have sold their tithes on account of want, and each village has taken action as a whole, the buyer should not suffer loss, but we will that some proper agreement be reached with him for the repayment of the sum by the village with due interest. But those who have tithes which they have not purchased from a village, but which were appropriated by their ancestors, should not, and ought not, to be paid anything farther by the village which shall apply its tithes to the support of the pastors elected as above indicated, or to solace the poor as is taught by the Scriptures. The small tithes, whether ecclesiastical or lay, we will not pay at all, for the Lord God created cattle for the free use of man. We will not, therefore, pay farther an unseemly tithe which is of man's invention.

The Third Article.—It has been the custom hitherto for men to hold us as their own property, which is pitiable enough, considering that Christ has delivered and redeemed us all, without exception, by the shedding of His precious blood, the lowly as well as the great. Accordingly, it is consistent with Scripture that we should be free and wish to be so. Not that we would wish to be absolutely free and under no authority. God does not teach us that we should lead a disorderly life in the lusts of the flesh, but that we should love the Lord our God and our neighbour. We would gladly observe all this as God has commanded us in the celebration of the communion. He has not commanded us not to obey the authorities, but rather that we should be humble, not only towards those in authority, but towards every one. We are thus ready to yield obedience according to God's law to our elected and regular authorities in all proper things becoming to a Christian. We, therefore, take it for granted that you will release us from serfdom as true Christians, unless it should be shown us from the Gospel that we are serfs.

The Fourth Article.—In the fourth place it has been the custom heretofore, that no poor man should be allowed to catch venison or wild fowl or fish in flowing water, which seems to us quite unseemly and unbrotherly as well as selfish and not agreeable to the word of God. In some places the authorities preserve the game to our great annoyance and loss, recklessly permitting the unreasoning animals to destroy to no purpose our crops which God suffers to grow for the use of man, and yet we must remain quiet. This is neither godly or neighbourly. For when God created man he gave him dominion over all the animals, over the birds of the air and over the fish in the water. Accordingly it is our desire if a man holds possession of waters that he should prove from satisfactory documents that his right has been unwittingly acquired by purchase. We do not wish to take it from him by force, but his rights should be exercised in a Christian and brotherly fashion. But whosoever cannot produce such evidence should surrender his claim with good grace.

The Fifth Article.—In the fifth place we are aggrieved in the matter of wood-cutting, for the noble folk have appropriated all the woods to themselves alone. If a poor man requires wood he must pay double for it (or, perhaps, two pieces of money). It is our opinion in regard to a wood which has fallen into the hands of a lord whether spiritual or temporal, that unless it was duly purchased it should revert again to the community. It should, moreover, be free to every member of the community to help himself to such fire-wood as he needs in his home. Also, if a man requires wood for carpenter's purposes he should have it free, but with the knowledge of a person appointed by the community for that purpose. Should, however, no such forest be at the disposal of the community let that which has been duly bought be administered in a brotherly and Christian manner. If the forest, although unfairly appropriated in the first instance, was later duly sold let the matter be adjusted in a friendly spirit and according to the Scriptures.

The Sixth Article.—Our sixth complaint is in regard to the excessive services demanded of us which are increased from day to day. We ask that this matter be properly looked into so that we shall not continue to be oppressed in this way, but that some gracious consideration be given us, since our forefathers were required only to serve according to the word of God.

The Seventh Article.—Seventh, we will not hereafter allow ourselves to be farther oppressed by our lords, but will let them demand only what is just and proper according to the word of the agreement between the lord and the peasant. The lord should no longer try to force more services or other dues from the peasant without payment, but permit the peasant to enjoy his holding in peace and quiet. The peasant should, however, help the lord when it is necessary, and at proper times when it will not be disadvantageous to the peasant and for a suitable payment.

The Eighth Article.—In the eighth place, we are greatly burdened by holdings which cannot support the rent exacted from them. The peasants suffer loss in this way and are ruined, and we ask that the lords may appoint persons of honour to inspect these holdings, and fix a rent in accordance with justice, so that the peasants shall not work for nothing, since the labourer is worthy of his hire.

The Ninth Article.—In the ninth place, we are burdened with a great evil in the constant making of new laws. We are not judged according to the offense, but sometimes with great ill will, and sometimes much too leniently. In our opinion we should be judged according to the old written law so that the case shall be decided according to its merits, and not with partiality.

The Tenth Article.—In the tenth place, we are aggrieved by the appropriation by individuals of meadows and fields which at one time belonged to a community. These we will take again into our own hands. It may, however, happen that the land was rightfully purchased. When, however, the land has unfortunately been purchased in this way, some brotherly arrangement should be made according to circumstances.

The Eleventh Article.—In the eleventh place we will entirely abolish the due called *Todfall* (that is, heriot) and will no longer endure it, nor allow widows and orphans to be thus shamefully robbed against God's will, and in violation of justice and right, as has been done in many places, and by those who should shield and protect them. These have disgraced and despoiled us, and although they had little authority they assumed it. God will suffer this no more, but it shall be wholly done away with, and for the future no man shall be bound to give little or much.

Conclusion.—In the twelfth place it is our conclusion and final resolution, that if any one or more of the articles here set forth should not be in agreement with the word of God, as we think they are, such article we will willingly recede from when it is proved really to be against the word of God by a clear explanation of the Scripture. Or if articles should now be conceded to us that are hereafter discovered to be unjust, from that hour they shall be dead and null and without force. Likewise, if more complaints should be discovered which are based upon truth and the Scriptures and relate to offenses against God and our neighbour, we have determined to reserve the right to present these also, and to exercise ourselves in all Christian teaching. For this we shall pray God, since He can grant these, and He alone. The peace of Christ abide with us all.

EXPLANATORY NOTES

EXPLANATORY NOTES *

1. *Wilhelm Zimmermann,* German historian and poet. Born January 2, 1807, in Stuttgart, in the family of an artisan. Graduated gymnasium in Stuttgart, studied in the University of Tuebingen together with F. Strauss. Was first pastor, then professor in the Polytechnic School of Stuttgart, occupying the chair of history, German language and literature. On April 23, 1848, he was elected representative of the National Assembly (Frankfurt). In St. Paul's Cathedral he joined the extreme left group of representatives. In 1850, he was deprived of the University chair for actively participating in the March revolution. In 1854, he renewed his activities as pastor in Zabergau. He died September 22, 1888.

As a historian, Wilhelm Zimmermann is known by his book, *The History of the Great Peasant War* (1841, 2d ed., 1856, 3d ed., 1891). Zimmermann left a series of works on history, history of literature, and poetry: *The History of the Hohenstaufens* (2d ed., 1865), *Illustrated History of the German People, History of Poetry of All Nations* (1847), etc.

The History of the Great Peasant War, Zimmermann's chief historic work, was written with astonishing mastery and objectivity. The author utilised documents and materials mainly of the Stuttgart archive. Generally speaking, Zimmermann's work remains the fullest presentation of the facts relating to the Peasant War. The objectivity of his presentation and "the revolutionary instinct which makes him an advocate of the oppressed classes" gives the book a special interest. But even in this book the radical bourgeois makes himself felt. Zimmermann's negative attitude toward socialism and communism does not allow him correctly to appreciate the conflict of classes in the history of the peasant wars.

Kautsky's book, *Forerunners of Socialism,* supplements that of Engels and corrects some inaccuracies in his presentation. The excerpts from Muenzer's speech which are quoted by Engels as parts of the sermon given before the princes of Saxony after the

* These notes were appended to the Russian edition of *The Peasant War in Germany,* edited by Prof. D. Riazanov.

167

destruction by the people of St. Mary's Chapel in Moellerbach, were written by Muenzer on an entirely different occasion in a polemic work against Luther. Engels here depends on Zimmermann.

Kautsky corrected Zimmermann in another more important question. Zimmermann depicts Muenzer as a man towering above his epoch. In his book, Kautsky proved this standpoint to be unfounded:

"Muenzer was superior to his communist followers, not by philosophical gifts and organisational talents, but by his revolutionary energy, and, first of all, by his statesmanlike mind."

Even some of the facts in the history of Muenzer's dictatorship in Muehlhausen, as given by Engels, need correction in some details. Muenzer was not at the head of the Muehlhausen council. Pfeifer was not his disciple, but a representative of a middle-class faction. (Franz Mehring.)

2. *Louis XI,* King of France, son of Charles VII. Born 1423, reigned 1461-1483. He founded the absolute monarchy on the ruins of feudalism in France, and extended the boundaries of his country to the Jura, the Alps, and the Pyrenees. In his youth, as dauphin, Louis participated in the uprising of the nobility against Charles VII. Having ascended the throne after the death of his father, he started a fight against the feudal lords but was opposed by the Common Welfare League which united the big and small feudal lords of France. In his wars against the League, Louis, instead of using the crude methods of feudal policies, practised not only force but cunning, a diplomatic system of lies, deception and caution. Louis XI was defeated and compelled to sign a peace pact with the feudal lords on October 29, 1461. But peace with the feudal lords was not achieved. Aided by the commercial class, he started a new war in November, 1470. All of western France rose against him, but this time he was victorious. In order to be able more successfully to oppose the feudal lords, Louis XI decided to reform the army by freeing the cities from military duties, and to create an army of 50,000. His infantry consisted of Swiss hirelings. In 1481, he added Provence and Liège to his domains and subdued the whole of France outside of Navarre and the duchy of Breton. The absolute power of Louis XI could establish itself in France only through the support of the commercial elements. Louis XI in his turn protected commerce, industry and agriculture. Under his reign the old institution of the Roman empire, the mail, was restored.

3. *Carolina,* a criminal code of the Sixteenth Century, published in 1532 under Emperor Charles V. In the Sixteenth Century, Germany counted over 300 states, each having its own criminal laws with its own methods of cruelty. Justice at that time aimed at

extorting a confession from the prisoner by means of torture. The prevailing Roman law, in the hands of the princes was a cruel tool for the exploitation of the people. The development of a money economy, however, and the growth of absolutism, demanded a uniform criminal legislation and a reform of the existing laws. Attempts at reform had been made in Germany as early as the end of the Fifteenth and the beginning of the Sixteenth Century. The Reichstag, meeting in Augsburg and Regensburg in 1532, finally adopted a draft of a criminal code known as Carolina ("Emperor Charles V's and the Holy Roman Empire's order of Penal Law"). This code did not abolish the Roman law, but was an attempt only to combine the prevailing Roman with the local law. Neither did the Carolina abolish the codes of the separate states, the new code serving only as a sort of guide for the princes and electors. The new code brought insignificant changes in the court procedure. It mitigated the inquisitional order of investigation and defined the right of defense. But torture as a means of examination of the defendant was retained in the new code. The chapters concerning the "cutting of ears," "cutting of noses," "burning," "quartering," adorned the new code as well. The code retained its great importance, however, up to the Eighteenth Century.

4. *Waldenses,* a religious sect which sprang up in the cities of southern France in the middle of the Twelfth Century. The cities of northern Italy and southern France of that time represented very favourable ground for the development of a religious reformist movement. Commerce and industry had developed here earlier than in the west; the bourgeoisie had come into existence, the crafts flourished. But while the cities of northern Italy, which were partly interested in the exploitation of Rome, since they derived from it no small profits, began to show spiritual independence only in relation to the doctrines of the Catholic Church, the cities of southern France, which were no less developed economically but at the same time less dependent upon Rome, started the first serious upheaval against the pope's domination.

According to the legend, the sect of the Waldenses was founded by a rich merchant of Lyons called Petrus Waldus. It is possible, however, that it existed prior to that time. Petrus Waldus decided to follow the law of the Gospel. He distributed his possessions among the poor, gathered around himself a considerable number of followers, and began preaching (1176). Soon the Waldenses combined in Lombardy with the sect of the Humiliates, who also called themselves the paupers of Lyons. The Waldenses did not confine their preachings to southern France. We find them also in Italy, Germany and Bohemia. In southern France, as elsewhere, they recruited their followers from among the artisans, particularly the weavers.

Originally, the Waldenses did not plan to secede from the church. But their free reading of the Gospel and their lay preachings, their disagreement with Catholicism in understanding the mysteries of transubstantiation, as well as their militant character, compelled the official authorities, the clergy, to start a campaign of cruel persecution against them. Pope Sixtus IV even declared a crusade against them in 1477. Those persecutions continued down to the Eighteenth Century. In 1685, French and Italian armies killed 3,000 Waldenses and captured 1,000. Only in 1848 did they attain civil rights and religious freedom in Piedmont and Savoy. Italian Waldenses are to be found even at present in the Alpine valleys, Val-Martino, Val-Angrona. The Twentieth Century finds 46 communities of Waldenses with 6,276 parishioners.

The Evangelist communism of the Waldenses in the Middle Ages was of a monklike character. For the "perfect" members of their community they made communism and celibacy obligatory. The "disciples," however, were allowed to marry and to possess property. The Waldenses rejected military service and the oath. They devoted their attention to the education of the masses. In those communities of the Waldenses where the peasants and the middle-class prevailed, they turned into a bourgeois-democratic sect. Where the proletarian elements prevailed, the Waldenses became communist "dreamers."

5. *Arnold of Brescia* made the first serious attempt to reform the Catholic Church as early as the middle of the Twelfth Century. Arnold of Brescia was born between 1100 and 1110 in Brescia, Italy. A disciple of the theologian and philosopher, Abélard, he adopted his critical attitude towards the religious dogmas and the teachings of the fathers. In 1136, he participated, with his native city, Brescia, in its struggle against its lord, the bishop. Arnold of Brescia strove to bring the clergy back to the real Christianity of the Gospel. He demanded that the clergy should relinquish lay authority and should hand over its possessions to the lay rulers. The clergymen who preached must content themselves with the tithe and voluntary contributions, he said. At the second Lateran church council (1139), the Bishop of Brescia accused him of heresy. Arnold of Brescia was compelled to flee to Paris. In 1146, he returned to Rome, where he participated in the struggle between the city democracy and the pope.

Rome in the middle of the Twelfth Century was a spiritual and political centre whither material wealth was flowing from all sections of the Christian world. The popes ably exploited the favourable situation of the Christian capital. Arnold of Brescia appealed to the people to depose the pope and to restore the ancient Roman republic. Pope Hadrian IV, however, succeeded in expelling him from the city. He was taken prisoner by Emperor Frederick Barbarossa and extradited to the authorities of Rome. He was hanged as a rabid heretic, and his body was burned (1155).

6. *The Albigenses,* a religious sect of southern France, were widespread in the Eleventh and Twelfth Centuries. Their name was derived from the city of Albi in Languedoc, one of the most important centres of the movement. The Albigenses preached apostolic Christianity and simple life according to the Gospel. They were called the "good men." The pope and the councils of the church claimed that they denied the Trinity doctrine, the Holy Communion and marriage, as well as the doctrine of the death and resurrection of Jesus Christ. At the council of Toulouse (1119), Pope Calixtus II, and subsequently in 1139 Pope Innocent II, excommunicated them. Finally, in 1209, Pope Innocent III organised a crusade against them. The war covered twenty years.

The stubbornness of the bloody fight against the Albigenses is explained partly by the fact that the Albigenses were aided in their war against the pope by the local feudal lords of southern France. When a papal legate and inquisitor was killed on the territory of Count Raymond VI of Toulouse, Pope Innocent III decided to use this occurrence as the occasion for taking away the lands from Count Raymond, who maintained a tolerant attitude towards the heretics. A struggle ensued between the lords of southern France and the pope, who was supported by the lords of the north. Northern France was in conflict with the south, which being economically more developed, was, therefore, a menace to it. The northern armies were headed by Count Simon de Montfort and papal legates. When the armies of the north took the city of Béziers, they killed 20,000 Albigenses. In the course of the ensuing struggle hundreds of thousands fell. The provinces of Provence and Languedoc were devastated. Peace was concluded only as late as 1229. In consequence of the wars against the Albigenses the wealthy south was destroyed and the territories of the French crown were expanded.

7. *John Wycliffe* (born October, 1320, died 1384), an English reformer. One of those ideologists who, even prior to the Reformation (Fifteenth and Sixteenth Centuries), drew an outline of the coming reforms. John Wycliffe was a professor of Oxford University. Prior to his appearance on the social and political arena, he devoted himself entirely to research work in the fields of physics, logic and philosophy. The Fourteenth Century was an epoch of stubborn fighting between the royal power of England and the

pope. The pope exploited England cruelly. In the Thirteenth Century, the English kingdom paid to the pope a yearly tribute of 1,000 pounds of silver. Under Edward III (Fourteenth Century), Parliament complained that the country was paying the pope a sum five times the amount of the taxes paid to the king. The development of industry and commerce increased the resisting power of England. The struggle between Rome and England was deepened by the Hundred Years' War between England and France (1339-1456). This war affected the interests of all classes of the English people. The governing classes of England sought possession of the treasuries of Netherland, and they also looked with a covetous eye on the riches of the French nobility. The middle-class saw in this war a means of enrichment. The burden of the war fell primarily upon the peasantry. It is not surprising, therefore, that the pope, having become an ally of France, aroused universal hatred in England. In 1336, Parliament abolished the tribute to the pope. Heresies persecuted in Italy and France now spread to England. Wycliffe's preachings were popular among all the strata of the people. He taught that in case of necessity the State had a right to deprive the Church of its possessions, that power was based upon service, and that consequently only service could justify the levying of taxes and duties by the clergy. In 1374, in disputes with the representatives of the Roman court, Wycliffe disclosed also the abuses of the Roman Church in appointing candidates to ecclesiastical posts in England. He was severely persecuted by the clergy, and only the interference of the court, and the intervention of the university and the cities, saved him.

In his doctrines, Wycliffe never overstepped the boundaries laid down by the ruling classes. He preached poverty and equality in Christ, but only for the clergy. He proposed that their lands should be expropriated; but this was entirely in the interests of the landowners and the king. The relations between man and God, Wycliffe pictured in the image of the feudal relations of his time. Man holds all his possessions, he said, from God. God's mercy is the condition of this vassalage. Mortal sin deprives man, he preached, of his right to hold possessions by the mercy of God. Therefore, he said, the clergy should have common property, and should submit to civil jurisdiction. The supreme judge of the human conscience, he said, was not the pope, but God.

After the peasant insurrection of 1381, a general sympathy for Wycliffe in his struggle against the pope changed into a hatred on the part of the propertied classes. Oxford University condemned his Twelve Articles, which rejected the doctrine of transubstantiation. Wycliffe died in peace, but his doctrines were cruelly persecuted.

In 1415, the church council at Constance decided to burn his remains.

8. With the name of *John Huss* is connected the struggle against the Catholic Church in Bohemia, the so-called Hussite movement of the Fifteenth Century. During the Fourteenth and Fifteenth Centuries, the Roman Catholic Church had lost its authority among the masses of the people. The Roman pope was, in the eyes of all peoples, an exploiter who deprived them of earthly goods in the name of God and heavenly life. In England, France and Spain, the Church was assuming a national character, severing its relations with Rome. The exception was Germany, which became the object of the avaricious appetite of the pope. If the other countries were in a more favourable condition, if they were earlier in a position to free themselves from under the papal yoke, it is to be explained only by the development of capitalism, the growth of wealth, and the power of the middle-class and the princes. Of all Germany, only Bohemia was, in this respect, in an exceptional situation. Bohemia developed economically in the Fourteenth Century with incredible rapidity because of its silver mines. The Church and the king with his court, as well as the merchants and the artisans, received enormous profits. The pope and the emperor were keenly watching Bohemia lest it free itself from their dependence. Dissatisfaction had begun to gather in the country. The lower nobility, the peasantry and the middle-class were dissatisfied. A price revolution, due to the abundance of silver, caused a general dearth. Besides, the masses of the people in Bohemia were Czechs, while the exploiting upper layer, the lay and ecclesiastical authorities, were Germans. Therefore the class struggle here assumed the character of a religious and national struggle of the Bohemians against the Germans and the pope. In this revolutionary medium, the ideas of the English reformist, Wycliffe, penetrated into Bohemia. Jan Huss was the literary defender and propounder of Wycliffe's ideas.

Huss was born in 1369, in a well-to-do peasant family. He was professor, and at one time rector, in the then famous Prague University, and also preacher in the Chapel of Bethlehem, where services were held in the Czech language. When the Prague University took a stand against the forty-five theses of Wycliffe, Huss came to their defence (1409). In 1412, Pope John XXIII, being in need of money, organised the sale of indulgences in Prague. Huss came forth with a heated sermon against the corruption of the Church, and demanded the termination of the traffic. He also opposed "miracles." In a special treatise, Huss proved that true Christians needed no miracles, and that true faith was contained only in the Holy Scriptures. Huss asserted that the Church was only an assembly of the faithful destined for Heaven, whereby he provoked the hatred of the ruling clique, who saw in the Church the dominance of the higher clergy.

On June 6, 1410, the books of Huss were burned, and he was excommunicated. In 1414, the Church council at Constance accused him of heresy, and though Huss declared that he wished to receive guidance and instruction from the princes of the Church as to wherein his opinions differed from the Word of God, he was turned over to the authorities and burned at the stake (June 6, 1415). His ashes were thrown into the Rhine.

9. *Hussites* (Taborites and Calixtines). The execution of Jan Huss set a revolution afoot in Bohemia. All the classes of the Bohemian people arrayed themselves against the power of the pope—for a church reform, and against the Germans—for national independence. In this nationalist religious struggle the masses of the people revealed their social hatred for the propertied classes. At the beginning, however, all classes of Bohemia acted in unison. The slogan of the struggle was the demand for communion under two forms. The rites of the Catholic Church gave to the layman in communion bread alone, and to the priests bread and wine. The masses rising against the privileges of the Church demanded equality in communion. "A chalice for the layman!"—that was the slogan of the movement. The nobility which joined the movement used this struggle to annex the lands of the Church; and the clergy held no less than one-quarter of the kingdom's territory. The rich bourgeoisie saw in the Hussite war also a means of gaining more riches from the clergy and the possessions of the German Catholic cities (Kuttenberg, with its famous silver mines was the most desirable of all). The nobility and the rich Bohemian bourgeoisie that joined the Hussite movement formed the moderate party of the *Calixtines* or *Utraquists*. Their centre was the city of Prague. Side by side with this moderate movement, however, there existed also a democratic one. Its bulk was formed by the peasants who wished to be free owners of the land, especially after the nobility had appropriated the land of the clergy. The lower middle-class of the cities and the proletarians were with the peasants. They were concentrated in the smaller cities of Bohemia. The democratic elements later began to call themselves Taborites after the name of their military and political centre, the communist city of Tabor. The Hussite movement was now headed by a group of communists.

In 1414, the people drove King Wenceslaus out of Prague, after which heretics began to flow into Bohemia from all parts of Europe.

The Beghards and the Waldenses found in Bohemia a refuge from persecution. The communists fortified themselves in Tabor where they started their propaganda. They declared that the Millennium of Christ had come, that there would be no more servants and masters, and that the people would return to the state of pristine innocence. In various cities, particularly in Tabor, the insurgents began to organise communist centres. Tabor was located in the vicinity of gold mines. Commerce and industry flourished there. When the communists became strong in Tabor they attracted large masses of the people. It is said that one gathering numbered 42,000 (July 22, 1419). The inhabitants of Tabor called each other brother and sister, and recognised no difference between "thine" and "mine." The Taborites taught that "there should be no kings, no masters, no subjects on earth, and that taxes and duties should be abolished." According to their doctrine there was to be no coercion, everything was to belong to all, and therefore, they said, he who possesses property commits a mortal sin. This communism, however, was of a Christian nature. It was a communism of consumption, not production. Every family worked for itself, contributing its surplus to the general treasury. There were among the Taborites the most extreme communists, who allowed no concessions, and denied the family. Those "brothers and sisters of the free spirit" called themselves Adamites. The majority of the inhabitants of Tabor and the knights, under the leadership of Zizka, launched a struggle against the Adamites.

The communist community of Tabor was surprisingly well organised. As a military community it alarmed the German princes for a long while. The Taborites represented the first regular army, and they were the first to use artillery in battle. That the Taborites could hold their own for almost a generation is explained by their attention to education, by the order and discipline in their community. Tabor fell, due, mainly, to a split among the Hussites. The moderate Calixtines, having appropriated the land of the clergy, did not wish to recognise the supremacy of Tabor. The war of the Taborites against the king, the pope, and all of Europe, was not in the interests of the nobility. After the victory of the Taborites at Tauss (1431), it seemed that there was no enemy capable of coping with them. But the Calixtines started negotiations with the enemy. They decided to call to a Diet all barons, knights, and representatives of the cities, to discuss a plan for a state organisation. Tabor itself was divided. The lower middle-class and the peasantry were indifferent to the communist programme. They wanted peace. Tabor's communism was not stable. It had not the foundation of communist production, therefore equality of the means of subsistence soon disappeared. There were both rich and poor in Tabor.

The army of Tabor was being overcrowded by "crooks and riff-raff of all nations." As soon as the nobility began to recruit soldiers for a war against Tabor, offering better conditions than the communist community, treason crept into the ranks of the Taborite army, and wholesale desertion began. This explains the fall of Tabor. On May 30, 1434, the Taborites suffered a crushing defeat near Czeski Brod. Out of 18,000 Taborite soldiers, 13,000 were killed. In 1437, they were compelled to conclude a treaty with Sigismund, who guaranteed them the independence of Tabor. But in spite of this the communist community of Tabor soon disappeared.

10. *Scourging Friars* (*Flagellants*)—a sect of people who whip themselves. It appeared in Europe as early as the Eleventh Century, and became widespread in the Thirteenth, Fourteenth and Fifteenth Centuries. From Italy, the movement spread through southern France, Netherlands, Alsace and Lorraine. The Flagellants taught that it was possible to obtain absolution from sin by inflicting sufferings on one's body. One of the first ecclesiastical theorists of this sect, George VII, taught that in this way the faithful emulated Christ, laboured to obtain a martyr's crown, deadened and castigated their flesh, and expiated their sins. This doctrine was in line with the prevailing asceticism of the Middle Ages, which demanded of the faithful to harden and torture their bodies by fasting, poor clothing, etc., in the name of Christ. The Flagellant movement, however, assumed the character of an epidemic, of a mass psychosis. Thus, in the Thirteenth Century, bands of people marched through the cities of Italy, whipping themselves with straps and lashes, and praying for absolution. After the devastating epidemic of the "Black Death," the movement assumed a dangerous character. In many localities of Germany, France and Flanders, Flagellants in mortal terror, imagining that Christ was about to destroy the world for the sins of mankind, inflicted cruel punishment upon themselves. In German cities, Flagellant communities began to come into existence. "Those desirous of partaking of self-castigation had to pay a small fee, and this was all demanded of proselytes." In the Fifteenth Century, the movement weakened, but it did not disappear. The Flagellants of the Fifteenth Century spoke evil of the monks and demanded a series of church reforms. The Roman Church, which at the beginning had not opposed the movement since, in Italy, it was anti-imperial and therefore a means of strengthening the Church, began to persecute the Flagellants. In the Sixteenth and Seventeenth Centuries, the movement became fashion-

able at court. Sex elements began to dominate in it. Traces of this sect can be found even in the Nineteenth Century.

11. *The Lollards* were a religious sect widespread among the working populations of England in the Fourteenth and Fifteenth Centuries. The heresies of those times found favourable ground not only among the master classes. As a matter of fact, every class formulated its demands through the reform movement. Thus, among the poorest weavers of England the sect of *Beghards,* or, as they were commonly called in England, Lollards, came into existence. (The Lollards were funeral chanters.) The Beghards first appeared in the Netherlands (Flanders and Brabant), in a country where commerce and industry had progressed earlier than in the rest of Europe and where sheep-breeding and the woollen industry were highly developed. The sect of Beghards was in most cases a fraternity of weavers. Unmarried artisans belonging to the sect lived in common houses, where they kept a communist household. The movement started in England when the weavers of Flanders migrated into that country. Norfolk, the centre of the woollen industry, became also the centre of the movement of the English Beghards, the Lollards. The Lollard propagandists, called "poor brothers," spread the new doctrine over the country. Errant "poor ministers" preached to the people that lay and ecclesiastical possessions should be common property. They urged the people to pay neither dues nor tithes to the clergy, and appealed to the servants to refuse to work for the masters. In 1395, the Lollards petitioned Parliament, demanding a reform of the Anglican Church, abolition of its worldly possessions and celibacy. The petition was rejected.

The most outstanding representative of the Lollards was John Ball, the mad minister of Kent. Coming from the ranks of the Franciscan monks who sympathised with the Lollard movement, he became one of the leaders of the peasant uprising of 1381 in England. Beginning with 1356, John Ball preached mainly in Essex and in Norfolk, delivering his sermons in city squares and cemeteries. They became very popular. He preached common property, and urged the people to exterminate the nobility. Only then, he said, would people be equal, and the masters would be no higher than the rest. All men originated from Adam and Eve, he said. "When Adam dolf and Eve span, who was then the gentleman?" he queried. He was killed during the suppression of the revolt in 1381.

The Lollard movement gained in importance when it became connected with the peasant uprising and with the opposition movement of the middle-class in the cities. After 1381, the Lollards found themselves in a precarious situation. Every Lollard was considered a criminal and treated accordingly. Terrorist acts against the sect continued for a long while, but it did not disappear from the lower strata of the working population, as is proven by pamphlets appearing even at the end of the Fourteenth and the beginning of the Fifteenth Century: "The Ploughman's Prayer" and "The Lanthorne of Light." The Lollards spread among the people a knowledge of the Bible in the English language.

12. *Chiliastic dreams, Chiliasm*—the doctrine of the second coming of Christ and the Millennium on earth. This Millennium was pictured as one thousand years of joy and happiness. All sufferings and privations, the adherents of this doctrine said, would disappear, and perfect harmony between mankind and rejuvenated nature would be re-established. The dreams of a Millennium became widespread in the Middle Ages, in years of elemental sufferings and socio-political cataclysms; in more quiet epochs, Chiliasm was the doctrine of small insignificant sects. Large masses of people were fired with Chiliastic dreams during the persecutions of the Christians in the Tenth Century, because the end of the world was expected to come in the year of Christ 1000. More widespread, however, were the Chiliastic dreams in the Fourteenth and Fifteenth Centuries, in the Reformation period. A back-to-the-Gospel movement, religious unrest, coupled with an increasing exploitation of the working population, were fertile soil for Chiliastic visions. Thomas Muenzer, the Anabaptists, and the Taborites, all paid tribute to the mystic doctrine of the Millennium.

Social conditions prevailing in the Middle Ages created an atmosphere favourable for mysticism. The ignorance of the masses nurtured it. Besides, Chiliasm, belief in miracles, and mystic visions were an outlet at a time when the masses saw no way of improving their condition by their own efforts. Only a miracle could, in their opinion, overthrow all oppressors and exploiters. The masses were driven to believe in the miracle of the second coming of Christ, in order that they should not sink into despair.

13. With the name of *Martin Luther* is connected the history of the religious and socio-political transformation of the Germany of the Sixteenth Century, the history of the so-called Reformation. Luther was not the initiator of that movement. His activities and doctrines by no means cover the social history of the Reformation. In the revolutionary movement of the Sixteenth Century, he was the representative of the coalition of the middle-class and the nobility.

From the Fourteenth to the Sixteenth Century, trade capital transformed the old natural economy of the European peoples, and rendered superfluous the political system of feudalism. The victory of absolutism became an economic necessity. On the other hand, development of commercial capital induced the masters to increase the exploitation of the peasants. Freeing the peasants from the feudal yoke, the masters increased their burdens, substituting cash payments for manual labour and payments in kind. The peasants were being driven off the land, and thus the nucleus of the future proletarian class was formed. This incipient proletariat was utilised by the army commanders and the merchants, by the former as material for the armies, by the latter as workers in their manufactories. In a period of economic revolution, feudal nobility became a hindrance to historic development. The lower nobility, the knights, took an intermediary position between the peasantry and the high nobility. The knighthood attempted to halt its own imminent ruin. In Germany, the struggle of these two class groupings was complicated by the peculiarities of German economic development. At the beginning of the Sixteenth Century, Germany, because of its mines and commerce, was still a powerful country economically. But the economic centre of Europe soon moved from the Mediterranean basin to the coast of the Atlantic. The development of Germany, as of all Eastern Europe, became stagnant. Under these circumstances well-established social and political conditions were either breaking down or changing radically. For a century Europe was shaken by terrific wars and revolutions. The exploitation on the part of the Roman Church was most keenly felt in Germany. The monasteries and the princes of the Church exploited the peasantry and the cities to the point of ruin. The middle-classes protested against the aid that the monasteries gave to the poor, because it limited them in their exploitation of the masses.

The Roman Church found a lucrative source of income in the sale of church offices and especially in the sale of the so-called *indulgences*—absolution for cash. The princes of the Church exploited the people in their own realm, as did the feudal land owners and the capitalist merchants in theirs. A struggle against the Roman Church became inevitable. But while England and France, economically more advanced than Germany, soon succeeded in freeing themselves from papal rule, Germany required a long and stubborn struggle.

In Germany, all classes of the population suffered gravely under papal exploitation, but each formulated its own programme. Luther's propaganda was the centre which originally united, first, the knighthood struggling against the princes, second, the lower clergy and the peasantry struggling against the princes of the Church and the feudal barons, and, third, the city middle-class chafing under the rule of the city aristocracy, the patricians.

Luther was born November 10, 1483, in a peasant family. His father worked in the mines. In 1501, he entered Erfurt University, where he led a very gay life in the circles of the Humanists, those advocates of radical ideas. In 1505, he entered a monastery, and, as every good Catholic, went to see the pope. In 1509, Luther gave a course of lectures in the Wittenberg University. In 1517, when Tetzel, the representative of Pope Leo X, opened a sale of indulgences in Saxony, Luther hung out on the doors of the Wittenberg chapel, his ninety-five theses against indulgences. His first protest against the Roman Church was very timid. Luther protested against corruption. Thesis 21 read: "Advocates of indulgences are mistaken when they say that through papal absolution a man is freed of all punishment." Thesis 27: "It is nonsense to preach that as soon as the penny jingles in the box, the soul leaves purgatory." Luther was surprised at the effect of his theses. He gave impetus to a movement which had started before him, and it engulfed all classes of Germany. Three groups became engaged in the struggle: the Catholic conservatives, the middle-class reformists, and the plebeian revolutionists. As a leader of the middle-class reformist movement, Luther at first appealed to violence, to the use of fire and iron for the extermination of the cancer that, he said, was destroying the world. He called for a decisive struggle against the lay and clerical princes. Between 1517 and 1522, Luther was ready to enter an alliance with the democratic factions. Between 1522 and 1525, however, he betrayed his allies, the peasantry and the lower clergy. His change was due to the Anabaptists in Zwickau and the peasant movement. He was also influenced by the uprising of the knighthood (Autumn, 1522).

At the head of the uprising of the knighthood were *Franz von Sickingen* and *Ulrich von Hutten*. The former was the commander, and the latter the ideologist of the movement. Their hatred for the pope and the princes and their striving for the reconstruction of a united Germany made them, by the middle of the Sixteenth Century, the heroes of the German bourgeoisie. In substance, however, the movement of united knighthood in a society where capitalism had begun to develop, was reactionary. Sickingen and Hutten dreamed of a renewed mediæval state where power was in the hands of the nobles and the emperor was their subject. They never aimed at freeing the cities or the peasantry, though they were compelled to appeal to them for aid. In the summer of 1522, Franz von Sickingen led troops against the "priestly nest" of Trier. But the armies of the united Rhenish and Suabian princes dealt him a decisive blow. Many castles were destroyed and many knights perished. Luther did not support that movement, but condemned it as well as that of the peasants.

In his first works, where he called the princes "the greatest fools on earth and the most heinous scoundrels," and in his first appeals relative to the Peasant War, Luther defended the insurgents. He wrote, for instance, "It is not the peasants who arose against you masters, but God himself, who wishes to punish you for your evil doings." Luther hoped to find in the peasant movement a support for his struggle against Rome. But when, in April and May, the peasantry revolted all over the country, burning and destroying castles, the movement assuming a communist character, Luther defended the princes against the insurgent peasants. He attributed the movement to the peasants' easy life. He urged the princes to "strangle them as you would mad dogs." When the insurrection was quelled, he bragged that he "had killed the peasants because he had given the orders to kill." "All their blood is upon me," he said.

An alliance was established between Luther and the princes, who were well satisfied with the acquisition of the church estates. The Reformation was profitable both to them and to the insurgents of the big cities. In 1526, at a Diet session in Speyer, it was for the first time decreed that the subject must follow the faith of his master. This saved the princes, who openly joined Luther. It is true that in 1529 Catholic services were reinstated and the confiscation of the lands of the clergy was halted in the provinces of the Lutheran princes, but the Lutheran minority protested against this decision—hence the name *Protestants*. In 1530, at a Diet session in Augsburg, the Protestant princes submitted to Emperor Charles V the so-called *Augsburg Confession* of the Lutherans. It consisted of two parts, the first giving an exposition of the new faith, and the second condemning the corruption of the Roman Church and outlining the necessary reforms.

"We reject those," says the Augsburg Confession, "who preach that absolution can be reached, not by faith, but by good deeds." Man can find favour in the eyes of God, says the document, only by the word of God and by the guidance of the Holy Spirit. We must not, it says, confuse the authority of the State with the authority of the pope; the Church has the power to preach the Gospel and to perform rites, but it should not participate in the affairs of the State.

The publication of the Augsburg Confession was not the end of the struggle. In September, 1555, at the Augsburg Diet, the so-called Augsburg Religious Peace confirmed the decision of 1526 relative to the obligation of the subjects to follow the faith of their masters. This decision made it obvious that Germany was to remain dismembered, under the rule of the princes. Lutherism became the religion of the economically backward countries. It spread in northern and western Germany, Denmark and Sweden, where the princes, the bishops and the landlords became the protectors of the Lutheran Church. But even this partial reform could succeed only as a result of the revolutionary movement of the peasantry, the cities and the knighthood.

14. *Joachim of Floris* (of Calabria) was an Italian mystic of the Twelfth Century. His doctrine of the *eternal gospel* is known under the name of Joachimism. In his conception, the Apocalypse teaches us that the world passes through three ages, the age of the Law, or of the Father, the age of the Gospel, or of the Son, and the age of the Spirit, which will bring the ages to an end. The first age, he said, corresponds to the Old Testament, the rule of lay authority, of external law and the preponderance of the flesh. The second age marks the predominance of the clergy, and the combination of spiritual and material interests. This, he said, was the age he lived in. The third age, he prophesied, would soon come and would be marked by a dominance of the spirit over the flesh, the monks becoming the ruling power, and the eternal gospel being the law of the world. Joachim denied that humanity was saved by Christ.

Joachim was of an urban family. Stricken by the horrors of the plague epidemic, he became a monk and founded the monastery of San Giovanni in Fiore. He wrote two books: *The Concordance Between the New and the Old Testaments* and *Commentary on the Apocalypse*. Several decades later (1260), the Joachimites were cursed by the pope and severely persecuted.

15. *Nicolas Storch* was a cloth-maker in Zwickau, where he became famous by preaching religious communism. Thomas Muenzer was under his influence and asserted that he knew the Bible better than all priests combined. In a short time, a whole community, which counted twelve apostles in its midst, gathered around Storch. His disciples believed that the truth was given to him in holy revelations. On May 16, 1521, the community of Zwickau invited a new preacher, Nicolas Hausmann of Schneeberg, a devoted friend of Luther's, and thus Storch's activities met with a stubborn opposition. He was expelled from the city, and went to the city of Wittenberg, where the "Zwickau prophets" hoped to find support in Carlstadt, a former co-worker of Luther. But they were compelled to flee to southern Germany where Storch dreamed of establishing the kingdom of God on earth. A holy revelation, he said,

made clear to him the true paths of social reformation. In 1522, Storch settled in Thuringia, where he became one of the initiators and leaders of the Peasant War. In collaboration with Muenzer, Pfeifer and others, he composed a programme of demands, which declared property to belong to all alike, since God had created all men equally bare and had given to them everything on the land, in the water and under the sky. All officers, lay and ecclesiastical alike, the programme said, must be removed from their offices, or killed. Every man could freely preach the law of God, as every one had a free will and was able to accept the good and reject the evil. Storch died in Munich in 1525.

16. *György Dózsa*—leader of the peasant insurrection of the Sixteenth Century in Hungary. At that time, the struggle between the absolute power of the king and the feudal lords of Hungary still continued. After the death of King Matthias, who, supported by the people, had conducted a successful struggle against the feudal lords, the latter regained the upper hand under Uladislaus, and abolished all the reforms of King Matthias including the standing army. The country was suffering under the struggles of the feudal lords. In 1514, the pope declared a new crusade against the Mohammedans. György Dózsa, who had become famous as a warrior in the fight against the Turks, was offered the post of commander. Within twenty days he gathered a people's militia numbering 60,000 men. Dózsa was the head of military operations. He was accompanied by two priests, who aroused the soldiers, peasants and city folk by their sermons. The feudal lords were loath to let their servants join the crusade, and, as harvest time was approaching, they demanded their return. In reply, Dózsa and the priests appealed to the people to rebel. The peasants arose all over Hungary, and the war with the feudal barons began. The situation of the peasantry in Hungary of that time was less intolerable than it was in the other countries, but having a little more freedom in Hungary, the peasants felt more keenly the yoke of serfdom. Incessant wars with the Turks were ruining the country. the population was being enormously depleted, and the peasants found themselves in a position to force upon the feudal lords a number of concessions. The peasants, however, being skilled in the art of war, hoped for full liberation. The lower clergy of the villages, hating the princes of the Church, joined the peasants. But they, along with the city middle-class, which also joined the peasant movement, soon betrayed it.

The leaders of the peasant uprising (1514) preached that the nobles were a criminal class which had enslaved the body and the soul of the peasant. They encouraged the destruction of the houses and the castles of the lords. György Dózsa, who had taught the peasants the use of arms, called them to rise all over the country. An army of feudal barons under John Zápolya moved against him. This army, aided by the city middle-class and the nobility, the former allies of the peasants, suppressed the movement cruelly. György Dózsa offered long and stubborn resistance. He proclaimed a republic declaring the power of the king and the privileged classes abolished. Notwithstanding the sympathy of the peasant masses throughout the country, György Dózsa was defeated at Temesvár. His execution was a refined torture. He was placed on a red hot iron throne, his head was adorned with a red hot iron crown, and a red hot iron sceptre was forced into his hand. Dózsa's only exclamation was: "These hounds!" No less than 60,000 peasants were killed in this uprising. The lords in Diet assembled, decided to increase the burden of the peasantry and declared serfdom a perpetual institution.

17. *The War of the Roses*—(1455-1485). After the termination of the Hundred Years' War between England and France (1339-1450) and after the English armies were compelled to evacuate France, a bloody war started between the two dynasties, Lancaster and York, which lasted over thirty years. The Lancaster dynasty, with a red rose as its emblem, represented the interests of the large feudal masters in Wales and in the north where their large estates were located. The York dynasty, with a white rose as its emblem, depended on the commercial southeast, the city population, the peasants and the House of Commons. The stubborn feud between the two dynasties was to decide whether England would become an absolute monarchy in case of the victory of the York dynasty, or whether it would be divided among the feudal masters with the victory of the Lancaster dynasty.

As early as the Fourteenth Century, large land possessions concentrated in the hands of a few noble families. In the Fifteenth Century, the House of Lords counted only one-third of its old members. The surviving dynasties annexed the land of those families that had disappeared. When the Hundred Years' War was over, the army was disbanded and the former soldiers taken into the service of the feudal masters. In the second half of the Fifteenth Century, the war between the two dynasties began. In the battle of Northampton (1460), York captured the king and compelled the House of Lords to recognise him as the protector of the state and the heir to the throne. He was defeated by the army of the hostile dynasty, but his son Edward returned to London victorious (1451). Edward's armies dealt mercilessly with the nobility. In the Taunton battle, forty-two knights and two lords were executed, while Warwick, one of Edward's commanders, saw to it that little harm was done to the Commoners.

The ascension to the throne of Edward IV, that is, the victory of the White Rose, marked the beginning of the period of absolutism. Edward IV did not raise the question of his election by the English Parliament. He expelled all feudal masters, even his closest friends who opposed his will (his fight against Warwick, "the maker of kings"). In his struggle against the feudal masters he used hired armies, thus making the feudal militia superfluous. He cruelly annihilated the adherents of the Lancaster dynasty. To make his victory secure, he refused to make new compulsory loans, and to secure the aid of the peasantry he demanded of Parliament laws prohibiting the dispossession of peasants. Thus the War of the Roses strengthened absolutism in England.

INDEX

A

Albigenses, 52, 54, 55, 171.
Alpine Region, 143.
Alsace, 140-142.
Anabaptists, 63; spreading Muenzer's doctrines, 71, 108.
Anspach, 109, 113.
Arnold of Brescia, 53, 54, 170-171.
Asceticism, plebeian, 74-75.
Augsburg, 34.
Augsburg Confession, 59, 181.

B

Baden, peasants' revolt of 1524, 101-103, 112-133.
Bakunin, on the Peasant War, 8.
Ball, John, 53, 55.
Baltringen Troop, 104, 106, 108, 118.
Bamberg, 109.
Beggar Kings, 82, 83.
Berlin, Hans, 123.
Bermatingen, 104, 118.
Bildhausen, peasant camp, 109.
Black Forest Hegau Troop, 104, 108, 124, 130.
Black Host (*Black Troop*), 110, 111, 113, 124, 127.
Breisgau, 88.
Bruchsal, 79-80.

C

Calixtines, 54, 55, 174-176.
Carinthia, 91, 143, 144.

Carniola, 91, 143, 144.
Carolina, the, 168-169.
Chiliasm, accepted by plebeian opposition, 56, 63, 178.
Christian Alliance, 107, 114.
Church, identifying its dogmas with political axions, 52; see also *Clergy*.
Cities, see *Middle Class*.
Clergy, aristocratic group of, 40-41; plebeian faction of, 41; retaining monopoly of education, 52; loss from Peasant War, 148.
Commerce, in early Sixteenth Century, 34-35.
Common Gay Troop, see *Gaildorf Troop*.
Conservative Catholics, 57.

D

Declaration of Twelve Articles, 112.
Dózsa, Geörgy, 89-91, 183-184.

E

Elector of Saxony, protecting Luther, 59.
Elector Palatine, 114, 121, 123.
Emperor Maximilian, 81, 150.
Engels, Friedrich, on Muenzer in 1845, 6; differing from Bakunin, 8; interest in Peasant War, 8-10.

187